Lift Heavy Sh*t

Menachem Brodie

Lift Heavy Sh*t: Intelligent Strength Training For The Masters Cyclist

Published by Fitness Marketing Group, Lake Ozark, MO

Printed in the United States of America

ISBN: 9798880165063

This publication is designed to provide accurate and authoritative information with regard to the subject matter covered. It is sold with the understanding that the publisher is not engaged in rendering legal, accounting, or other professional advice. If legal advice or other expert assistance is required, the services of a competent professional should be sought. This book is for informational purposes only. It is not intended to substitute the practices of your doctor, dietician, or other health care provider. It is up to you to do your due diligence to collaborate with your personal health care providers.

First edition

For more information, contact:

Brodie@HumanVortexTraining.com

Visit us online at: www.HumanVortexTraining.com

Table of Contents

Introduction

Over the last 20 years, there has been a dramatic shift happening in our lives, in that we are now expected to live longer than any previous generation. Our life expectancy has been drastically lengthened thanks to advances in our understanding of how the human body works, what we need to do to keep it healthy and in good working order, as well as advances in science, technology, and modern life.

As the rock group, Rush sang:

> *"A modern-day warrior*
>
> *Mean, mean stride*
>
> *Today's Tom Sawyer*
>
> *Mean, mean pride"*

Well, for many the *"mean, mean pride"* is that of being fit, healthy (having gotten there somewhere between their college years and today, or those for whom it has been a lifelong undertaking), and having the desire and will to see just how strong and fast they can get.

While we have seen the opinions and thoughts about strength training for cyclists (and triathletes) turn from *"lift light weights for high reps to improve your endurance"* to the current rallying cry of *"Lift Heavy Sh*t,"* there are some basic foundations which have been completely skipped over, or which have been neglected to be mentioned.

Like most, you probably jumped into lifting heavy weights hoping it would help you ride stronger, rid you of achy knees, hips, and lower back, and get down to a leaner riding weight.

But many riders, just like you, have jumped on this new, *"science-backed"* approach, with enthusiasm, excitement, and expectation, only to be left with a body that feels horrible for days after these strength training sessions. You fear the stairs (any stairs), cannot even think about pedaling your bike because it feels so bad, and are left wondering what the heck you're doing.

How are these strength training sessions, that leave you sore and crushed for a few days after (sometimes even making your lower back, hips, and knees more achy than they were before) supposed to help you ride better?

This is why so many riders drop their strength training at the first excuse that comes along:

"My ride volume went up this week, I don't really have time for strength training."

"My legs are too sore to pedal my bike, and I feel like I'm getting worse on the bike…Strength training has to go, I'm a cyclist, dang it!"

"I'm too tired to do my strength, besides, I need to ride my bike to get faster on it!"

If you've thought or said any of these, or any other reason why *"lifting heavy"* needs to go so you can ride your bike more, you are correct!

The way that lifting heavy sh*t has been dived into, with utter reckless abandon, is in fact draining you of your abilities to ride your bike.

The science is wonderful, as it is helping the average rider and their coach to understand that heavy lifting does in fact improve your riding abilities and needs to be included in your regular training program.

But, and this is a huge but, it does not tell you *how* to properly incorporate it.

You see, the researchers job is to isolate one thing, the thing which they are studying, in order to determine if their hypothesis is true. And if it is true, why.

That's it.

Failure to isolate the specific thing, means their research outcome will be questionable and unreliable.

But while this process is important for us to drive forward our understanding of the why, it does nothing to help you understand how to implement the information in a way that helps you improve in a sustainable fashion.

And that is where this book comes in, to help you be able to progress and develop as both a cyclist and a strength training cyclist.

So if you've been hitting the weights, lifting heavy sh*t, all the while having this suspicion or gut feeling that *"there has to be a better way,"* you are 100% right.

There is.

And the very book you are holding in your hands is it.

It's time to push back against the reckless, teenager-like rallying cry of *"Lift heavy sh*t! It's what the research says you need to do!"*

Actions have consequences, and as you've probably already felt, we are no longer in our teens or twenties, where we can easily absorb and bounce back from those brutal trainings in a short time.

Yes, we do need to lift heavy sh*t, but we need to do so with the wisdom that comes with experience of working with real humans in their day-to-day lives, not within the confines of a research study over 8-12 weeks completed on 20-something neo-professionals.

That is what you will learn in this book.

HOW to lift heavy, in a way that not only allows you to ride faster, stronger, and more powerfully, but that also helps you to improve your posture, move better, and feel better than ever.

But before we go any further, it is important to make clear who this book is for.

If you are someone who enjoys an occasional bike ride here and there, but want a program that will help you strength train and get really strong in the weight room, but you are not really concerned about how fast or strong you ride your bike, this book is **not** for you.

You'll be much better off picking up and implementing *Easy Strength*, by Dan John.

If you are a female looking to learn more about perimenopause or menopause and the various changes that are happening and how to use strength training as one of the various items to help you address those changes and *"fight back,"* this book *might* be for you.

But if you're looking for detailed menopause and perimenopause specific strategies and approaches to use, this book is **not** for you. We'll cover the information you need in order to lift heavy stuff sustainably, but we will not be diving into the menopause specific issues and items.

You'll want to pick up and implement *Next Level: Your Guide To Kicking Ass, Feeling Great, and Crushing Goals Through Menopause and Beyond* by Dr. Stacy Sims.

This book is, however, a great accompaniment to Dr. Sims' book and can significantly help you get the most out of your time and efforts with weights.

Who Is This Book For?

This book is for cyclist (and triathletes), both women and men, especially those 50+, who have heard the rallying cry of *"lift heavy sh*t,"* but pause, recognizing that there is something missing... Those who understand jumping into heavy lifting and expecting magic to happen is more like trying to catch the Road Runner; it just does not end well (more on Mr. Wile E. Coyote to come later).

This book is for those cyclists and triathletes who are looking for a proven path to using strength training to help them get not only faster and more powerful on the bike, but to feel, look, and move better off the bike.

To raise their quality of life a level or three, by adding strength training to their weekly healthy habits in a way that is enjoyable, progressive, helps them feel better (not smash you to bits every strength training session), and is sustainable.

So if you want to learn how to lift heavy sh*t from someone who has been teaching it for over 20 years, who is also an accomplished cycling and triathlon coach, who understands the demands that both of these worlds are placing on you, and who has helped literally thousands of riders just like you since 2007 to tap into the seeming *"fountain of youth"*. . . Then this is *__the__* book for you.

I'm glad you are here and am excited to share with you the very principles and approaches that can have you riding stronger than you did at 30, feeling just as good as you did at 20, but with the wisdom and experience to make it even more powerful and enjoyable.

Let's get started.

Chapter One

Masters Of The Game

As a seasoned cyclist over 50, your experience on the bike has likely brought you many rewarding adventures and challenges. However, as we age, our bodies undergo natural changes that can impact our performance and overall well-being. This is where the importance of strength training comes into play, especially for more seasoned and experienced riders, who have not included regular year-round strength training in their training routines.

In this chapter, we will delve deeper into the unique needs and considerations for strength training as a seasoned cyclist over 50, helping you maintain your passion for cycling and continue to push your limits using strength training and lifting "heavy stuff" to help you tap into the fountain of youth.

1. The Importance of Strength Training for Riders Over 50

There are several different reasons we get into cycling: for some it's an opportunity to get out and explore, and for others it's a necessary change due to cranky hips or knees thanks to the miles we've put in running or playing ball sports in our younger years. Cycling is a fantastic way to build a healthier heart, lunges, and overall cardio health, however it does not help to build stronger muscles and bones.

Add to this the fact that aging naturally leads to a loss of muscle mass and bone density through a process, known as sarcopenia, and we have a recipe that can cause decreased strength, power, and endurance - factors crucial for cycling and living a healthy, active life.

Strength training can counteract these age-related changes by stimulating muscle growth, improving tissue strength, recruiting more of your nervous system, and improving bone density. By enhancing your strength, you can better engage key muscle groups involved in cycling and improve your overall performance on the bike.

As the saying goes: *"Use it or lose it."*

For masters riders, there are really 3 primary goals we want to get out of your strength training:

1. Improved Movement Quality

2. Connective Tissue Strength

3. Increased Work Capacity

These will allow you to not only look and feel better but also to be stronger, more powerful on the bike, and more resilient in your abilities to train, ride, and tackle whatever life throws your direction.

Most masters athletes I work with, whether they are looking to win their age group of an event, or just want to ride pain free while looking and feeling great, come in thinking that they need to immediately *"lift heavy $h*t"* or "increase power and force production through strength training".

While these are great goals, once we get moving towards the 3 primary goals we just mentioned, those items, along with many of their performance goals, are checked off.

Not that increasing force production and power output shouldn't be your goals... but rather that these are more often than not, achieved when we put our focus into these 3 items, in this order.

Getting What You Want And Need From Your Strength Training

Number one: We need to make sure you move well.

Your hinges (deadlifts) look like hinges.

You can push and pull while keeping core control and move well from the shoulder.

You can move freely and with good control through the ball and socket joints of the hip and shoulder, while keeping core stiffness.

Your squats look like squats.

And that you can appropriately deal with the deceleration forces before we get into jumping, and your tendons are ready for the tasks and demands of jumping & landing.

If you do not move well, the load we can put on you is going to be limited.

This leads into number two: Connective Tissue Strength.

We start off improving your connective tissues on day 1 of your strength training program by using our 3-1-3-1 Tempo (you'll learn what this is in Chapter 4) where you're learning how to move well and we are placing focused stresses on the connective tissues to adapt.

Both of these first two goals build beautifully into our third goal of Building Work Capacity.

As you get better at your movements, we can do more repetitions (adding volume) which helps drive the very adaptations of the connective tissue, muscles, fascia, and nervous system that we are after.

All the while, we are trying to increase the variability of movements and the stresses on the tissues in the body.

This is incredibly important, and one of the missed keystones when well-meaning coaches give you "moves that look like cycling" for your strength training.

You already get tens of thousands of repetitions on the bike for those movements, and they are the last thing you need!

What you truly need is to improve your body's ability to move well, place different stresses on the body that will help you to better deal with the various forces and work you do on the bike, and that will help your body to stay strong, resilient, and move well now, and for decades to come.

2. The *"Common Knowledge"* Myth: Targeting Muscle Groups for Cyclists

For many years, it has been mistakenly believed that in order to maximize your cycling abilities, it's important to focus mostly on specific muscle groups during strength training sessions that work when you're riding your bike. The muscles that have often been focused on include:

- **Quadriceps**

- **Hamstrings**

- **Glutes**

- **Calves**

- **Core Muscles**

And for the more forward-thinking folks, they'll also consider:

- **Upper Body Strength**

While this segmented, muscle by muscle approach to movement *seems* like a good idea, it actually misses a vital and very basic keystone of human movement:

Nothing moves by itself.

The 3 Jobs of a Muscle

In fact, a muscle has 3 jobs in the body:

1. To protect a joint from injury

2. To stabilize a joint while an adjacent joint moves

3. To move a joint

Every skeletal muscle of the body will work in this fashion, and following this order of operation.

Muscles will tighten to protect a joint from injury, due to either instability or a lack of balance/tuning through the system of movement. Muscles will also tighten if a muscle further up or down in the system is weak or otherwise out of place and unable to do their job appropriately. We'll get into that a bit more in Chapter 6.

This notion of muscle by muscle workouts came from the Western approach to training and fitness, which was heavily influenced, if not led, by the bodybuilding world.

While these approaches do not work well when one is seeking to build better athletic performances or towards longevity and vitality in their lives, they were a necessary step in evolution of strength training for the masses in Western culture to help us add strength training into the conversation about health.

The likes of Jack LaLane, Arnold Schwartzenneger, and Fred Hatfield helped to spread the gospel of strength training. As such, much of the information and approaches we have learned as a society in the west are based on bodybuilding.

There is nothing inherently wrong with body building. It is an incredibly challenging, and oftentimes fun, approach to pushing one's muscles to grow.

But it is about as far from performance and longevity training as one can get.

Having met and spent considerable time with former IFBB Bodybuilding professionals and "regular gym goers," I can tell you beyond a shadow of doubt, that bodybuilding unequivocally does more to break the body down in the long run, than build it up.

Knee, hip, and shoulder replacements are very common, as bodybuilders look to maximize strain on the muscles themselves, often at the sacrifice of safe and efficient mechanics.

But if you're seeking to improve your health, increase your ability to move well for many years, gain strength, and boost your performance in any sport, you **must** change your focus from training muscles to _training movements_. . . And learning to move well.

Meet Then Unknown Workhorse of Movement: The Fascia

Training movements allow you to target the all-important and ever-present tissue called the Fascia. While we are only recently beginning to understand how integral and intertwined fascia is in the human body (it's much like a spiderweb that runs through each and every muscle in your body), we have come a relatively long way in a short time.

If fascia sounds familiar, it's probably because since the early 2000s we've had many runners and triathletes talk about the Plantar Fascia, as these populations have often had issues with this area. But the fascia does not act in a part to part or muscle to muscle way. Fascia run in what are often referred to as _"lines"_ or _"meridians"_ in the body, connecting muscles and areas which to the average Joe doesn't believe have any connection to each other.

Let's look at an example:

Going with the Plantar Fascia, which is on the bottom side of your foot, that fascia is actually a part of a line that runs up the backside of your body, through the calves, hamstrings, hip rotators, your lower back, your trapezius (mid- back muscles) up your neck and the backside of your head, and attaches at the muscles that move your eyebrows!

It is all one continuous system which works together and affects one another. And that is just one of several lines of fascia in your body!

Another pair of fascial lines which greatly affects us as cyclist are the "Anterior Oblique Sling" and "Posterior Oblique Sling". These fascial slings act as force transferring systems.

These two slings work in chorus with each other to provide core stability (along with other fascial slings in the body) by compressing the pelvis, which comprises 3 bones (the Sacrum and the two iliac bones {Ileum}) to allow you to produce power and movement from the hip.

It's not your leg muscles that allow you to produce power down to the pedals from the hip, it is the fascial system working together as a part of whole-body effort to create stiffness where you need it in the right amounts, so that you can get movement.

The above mentioned Anterior Fascial Sling (on one side) includes the muscles of your transverse abdominis (TVA), internal and external obliques on the one side (those muscles under the "love handles"), and the pectorals (chest muscles) on the opposite side.

The Posterior Fascial Sling (on one side) includes one of your hamstring muscles (bicep femoris), the same side glute max (your big outer butt muscle), and the other side latissimus dorsi (that big V shaped muscle Arnold is famous for).

These fascial lines run all through your body, and tie your upper body and lower body together in an inseparable fashion, which requires a more holistic view of human movement in order to better prepare the body for sport and performance.

Hopefully now you understand why ignoring your upper body and/or treating it as an afterthought in your strength training is a huge, massive mistake, just as looking at each muscle as a singular entity is selling you up the strength training and cycling river without a paddle.

But if we shouldn't look at our strength training in a muscle by muscle fashion, how should you break down your workouts?

By movements.

Let's take a look at what I call the "FUN-damental 5+1 Movements", as these form the very foundation of what we want to accomplish through your strength training: Moving extremely well, with strength, and being able to *"lift heavy $h*t"* for these 6 primary movements in some fashion.

The Fun-Damental 5+1 Human Movements

- Push

- Pull

- Squat

- Hinge

- Press

- Rotary Stability

And, if we want to build a truly robust and durable body:

- Carry

If you've read my first book *Strength Training for Cycling Performance*, I housed carries under the Rotary Stability label. But because we are specifically talking about strength, performance, and longevity here, we must separate carries out as their own category, due to the huge benefits they offer you in daily tasks and overall strength and durability.

3. Flexibility and Mobility for Cycling

In addition to strength, flexibility and mobility are crucial for optimizing your cycling performance. Regularly performing exercises through range of motion with good technique and mobility drills can improve your range of motion, minimize muscle imbalances, and enhance your pedaling efficiency.

As perfectly cited in the book, "Principles & Practice of Resistance Training,"

"Strength, in and of itself, is one of 5 interrelated characteristics of fitness that we need to improve if we want to be stronger, fitter, and healthier in order to add longevity and vitality in our years."

The five properties are:

1. Speed

2. Endurance

3. Flexibility

4. Strength

5. Skill

These properties all blend with one another depending on the chosen sport and its demands. Understanding that each sport that can be done on a bicycle requires a completely different blending of these characteristics is key!

A cross-country mountain biker has very different demands on them than trail riding and enduro. A gravel rider has a different skew than the cross-country mountain biker, and so on.

The changes of the properties blending together occur not only due to the types of technical skills one needs but also due to the bike, terrain, the speeds, and the equipment the rider will be required to use.

These differences in the profile of each sport will significantly impact how much mobility & flexibility you will need, and in what areas, based on which kind of riding you are mostly doing for a period of time.

Having appropriate and good mobility & flexibility is important, as it allows the tissues to move better, airflow and blood flow to happen more easily, as well as allowing the body to move efficiently and effectively deal with the forces being placed on it.

- **Stretching:** Dynamic stretches, such as leg swings and hip rotations, can warm up your muscles before rides and improve joint mobility. Static stretches, when done after workouts, can help muscles return to their pre-ride resting length. As you'll learn, while static stretching can have a place in a program, especially as we get into our 5th decade and beyond, breathing and dynamic stretches can often have an even better impact on your health & mobility, with results that are much longer lasting.

- **Foam Rolling:** Incorporating self-myofascial release techniques with a foam roller, tennis ball, lacrosse ball, or medicine ball, can help alleviate muscle tension and enhance tissue flexibility through more targeted focus of the self-massage. Massage guns have gained popularity the last few years, however due to the intensity that these tools operate at, and the fact that massage does cause tissue breakdown, I do not usually recommend them. When foam rolling, focus on areas such as the quadriceps, tensor fascia latta, glutes, calves, upper back, lats, and chest.

- **Mobility Drills:** Exercises like arm swings, lunge reach twist, and Spidermans (also called *"the greatest stretch"* or *"groiners"*) can improve joint mobility and increase your body's ability to adapt to different cycling positions and movements, as well as help you to unwind some of the imbalances and postures that often happen when riding our bikes for long periods of time.

4. The Role of Periodization

Periodization is a training approach that involves dividing your training into distinct periods or phases to maximize results and prevent plateauing. This approach can be especially beneficial for seasoned cyclists over 50.

In our 20s and 30s, it tends to be much easier to absorb and roll through a riding season, allowing ourselves to push hard all summer, and then use the late fall and winter to "recover" from our big ride time. But as we get into our 40s and beyond, this may be a "fun and easy" approach, but it is also the fast-track to knee, hip, and lower back pains, as well as seeing our abilities on the bike decrease, thus slowing us down. The bike beats you up more than it adds to the enjoyment to your life, and it seems the hands of time are pulling you back and down.

But there is another way that we can look at your riding season that can not only help you ride strong year to year but also help you build your fitness year on year!

Consider implementing the following periodization framework for your riding year:

- **Base Phase:** Focus on endurance and strength-building exercises. This phase helps lay the foundation for the rest of your training by improving your aerobic capacity and overall strength.

- **Build Phase:** Increase the intensity and volume of your strength training exercises. This phase aims to build muscle and improve your ability to generate power on the bike.

- **Peak Phase:** Maximum enjoyment on the bike, either via a goal event, trip, or prime-time of year. This phase aims to allow you to be at your strongest of the year, and to feel great while either riding long, fast, or both! This period can last anywhere from 3-14 days, depending on your level of experience and fitness

- **Maintenance Phase:** Once you've peaked at your desired level of riding strength and power, switch to a maintenance phase focused on maintaining your gains and Enjoying your higher levels of fitness. However, there should be a slight drop off from your peak-form bests. This phase should last no longer than 3-4 weeks.

- **Transition Phase:** Gradually shift your focus away cycling-specific exercises and activities. If you've been on a road bike 80%+ of the main season, try mountain biking, or even better, do something completely different from cycling for a few weeks to give the mind and body a break.

What about being "Perma-Fit?"

For many of us as Masters, but not competitive athletes, we can fall into the trap of trying to be *"perma-fit."*

This term just means that you want to be in good shape year-round.

There is nothing wrong with aiming to be perma-fit, but it comes with sacrifices...

As the saying goes, *"you cannot have it all."*

This is especially true when it comes to fitness and performance.

As we add birthday candles to the cake each year, we tend to lose the drive to push outside of our comfort levels, as our internal drive to compete with others tends to lose its edge a bit.

Joe Friel talks about this in his book *"Faster After 50,"* as it is one of the contributing factors why we tend to avoid the shorter, really hard (and painful) efforts... but this is also where a lot of our gains and improvements for our health and fitness live!

This is where perma-fit may seem like a good idea, but in reality, in order to stay healthy and well, you need to have an ebb and flow in your riding and training.

> *"If you're not growing, you're dying."*
> - Tony Robbins

Rather than riding at the same level all year, for every 6-month period, aim to incorporate 3-4 weeks where you really push a specific effort type, or certain kind of terrain.

These few weeks of focused effort can not only help you improve your fitness year to year but also allow you to unlock new skills and tools that you haven't tapped into before, as well as help you build a better, more robust YOU.

While you may not be training for a specific event or trying to reach peak fitness, the bottom line is that in order to stay healthy and strong, we, as human beings, need times of stress to drive the adaptations needed to gain fitness or improvements.

5. Incorporating Strength Training into Your Cycling Routine

One of the biggest challenges for cyclists is changing their mentality from strength training being an "add-on" or "base period" activity, to understanding that strength training must be done consistently, year round, in order to gain the results and benefits to be healthier, move better, and ride stronger, including, but not limited to:

- Improved bone density & health

- Improved tendon health

- Improved power output on the bike

- Improved recovery between rides

- Improved posture

This year- round approach means that throughout your riding season the focus of your strength training will change as the time on the bike, and the focus of your riding changes. There are five stages throughout the year, four of which you'll move through, with the fifth being only for those who have a true single peak event within a season.

1. Anatomical Adaptations

2. Hypertrophy

3. Max Strength

4. Specialization/ Sport Specification

5. Maintenance

Let's take a look at what each stage offers you in order to allow you to strength train year round while building a better moving, looking, and feeling body.

1. **Anatomical Adaptations**
   Helps you improve movement by working on preparing tissues for loading, working on active mobility, and unwinding tight spots developed through the season

2. **Hypertrophy**
   Builds muscle cross-sectional strength in a way that allows you to get far stronger through the muscles, tendons, bones, and for nervous system recruitment, while improving stability

3. **Maximum Strength**
   Develops abilities of the nervous system to recruit maximum motor units, improvement in ability to move with force and efficiency

4. **Sport Specification (Conversion to Sport)**
   Develops speed, power, and transition strength to in-sport skills such as climbing, sprinting and braking/cornering.

5. **Maintenance**
   Touching on movement patterns in a way that decreases the loss of strength and/or movement improvements made in the months leading up

The Argument Against Periodization

While there are some in the cycling world who believe that one cannot periodize strength training due to our sports long seasons and ever changing demands, this is a mistaken thought. Although I definitely understand where they are coming from, what they are missing is the term "Classical approach" of periodization.

We'll dive more into this topic in Chapter 8's subtopic *"To Periodize, or Not To Periodize... That Is Not Even A Question!,"* as there is a journey we need to take first of building a high-resolution mind map (or a mental picture, if you prefer), that will help you better be able to critically think about the topic.

General Overview Of A Training Year

Here is a sample of what the strength training year will look like for those living in the northern hemisphere pairing the cycling periods, with the strength periods, starting with the end of the season (fall):

October:
Transition (on-bike) + Anatomical Adaptations (Strength)

November-January:
Base (on-bike) + Hypertrophy (Strength)

February-April:
Late Base into Early Build (on-bike) + Max Strength (Strength)

May-June:
Build (on-bike) + Sport Specification (Strength)

July:
Peak (On-bike) + Maintenance (Strength)

August- September:
Maintenance (on-bike) + Max Strength/ Hypertrophy (Strength)

You'll notice that following the year-round strength training programming, you are lifting *"heavy"* during the riding season. This goes against *"Common knowledge,"* but as you'll soon learn here, it actually makes sense, and offers you massive rewards, when done well.

To effectively integrate strength training into your cycling routine, consider the following factors:

- **Frequency:** Ideally, we are aiming for at least two days of strength training per week, up to three, allowing for adequate recovery between sessions. While there may be times where four days in a week can serve a purpose, those times tend to be few and relatively far apart, unless you have been strength training for many years continuously, without a drop of longer than 2-3 months.

- **Duration and Intensity:** When we're looking to strength training to improve cycling, your sets and repetition ranges will change throughout the training year.

- **Training Modalities:** Mix up your strength training routine by incorporating bodyweight exercises, resistance training with weights or bands, and plyometric exercises to improve power and explosiveness.

- **Rest and Recovery:** Allow for ample rest and recovery time between strength training sessions to give your muscles time to

repair and grow. This will prevent over-training and reduce the
risk of injury.

6. Proper Nutrition and Recovery

Finally, to support your strength training goals and optimize your overall
performance on the bike, focus on nutrition and recovery. Ensure you
consume a well-balanced diet rich in lean proteins, complex carbohydrates,
and healthy fats to provide your body with the necessary nutrients for
muscle repair and growth. Hydration is also critical, especially during
intense workouts and longer rides. Adequate rest, sleep, and stress
management techniques are equally important for ultimate recovery and
maximizing the benefits of strength training.

By considering these unique needs and considerations for strength training
as a seasoned cyclist over 50, you can enhance your cycling abilities,
prevent injuries, and maintain peak performance. With focused training,
a commitment to overall fitness, and the inclusion of periodization and
proper nutrition, you can continue to push your limits and enjoy the
exhilarating world of cycling for years to come.

Chapter Two

The Science of Ageless Strength

Unpacking the physiological benefits of intelligent strength training and its impact on longevity.

The human body is an intricate system, with various interconnected parts working together to sustain life. When looking at how to improve performance or health, these intricate systems boil down to 4 foundational systems that work together to allow us to be healthy, and function well as a human being to create what Performance Coach Joel Jamieson describes as "Biological power" in his book *Ultimate MMA Conditioning*:

1. Hormonal (endocrine) System

2. Cardiovascular System

3. Neuromuscular System

4. Metabolic System

Should one of these 4 pillars be neglected or not kept "up to par", our fitness and health will begin to suffer. Or, as Joel explains:

"The greater the biological power you are capable of, the higher your level of work capacity will be as a whole and the more training you are able to adapt positively to.

The reason for this is because it takes a lot of energy to adapt to the high level of physical and mental stress that your body goes through as a result of training. After each training session, your body must go through the difficult job of repair and recovery of many different tissues. Sugar stores have to be replenished, hormonal levels have to be restored to normal, muscle tissue needs to be repaired, etc."

In essence, the more biological power you are able to produce, the faster your recovery and adaptation to a given training stress will be. However, this is where many masters cyclists go off-track with their training programs... They only perform strength training during "the winter" or "base period," leaving their biological power to be greatly lacking from the neuromuscular standpoint.

This lack of regular, consistent training from a strength standpoint has a trickle down effect on the metabolic and endocrine systems, which slows your recovery and adaptation down even more.

It is this very fact, that most masters cyclists leave strength training to be performed only for a small piece of their training year, which leads to the *"age slowdown"* or *"I'm getting older, so getting slower is just part of that process."*

The difference between seeing faster times, or having the same power feel easier to produce, comes almost exclusively from how well you develop each of these four systems to work together.

As you'll learn in the coming chapters, there is a lot of misunderstanding about when and how to lift "heavy" throughout the cycling season and annual calendar.

Some of what we will discuss may contradict what you've heard or seen as "common knowledge" practices, but once you've tried it and see the results for yourself, you won't go back.

The Fountain of Youth

Within this complex web of physiology, the lower back and hips hold a prominent position. They serve as vital foundation points, supporting our posture, enabling movement, and ensuring the overall health and longevity of our bodies. Understanding the significance of these areas and their role in strength training is essential for achieving ageless strength and reaping its benefits.

In fact, within the "fountain of youth" that is strength training, one might say that better understanding the role of the spine and hips, and how to best use them for pain free, healthy movement and power production, is the "secret sauce."

Intelligent strength training transcends the realm of muscle building and aesthetics, delving deep into the science behind how it positively influences our physiology and improves your movement habits throughout your day-to-day life.

By focusing on strengthening the muscles surrounding the lower back and hips, and learning how to move in a more spine-friendly and spine-sparing fashion, we can unlock the secrets to maintaining health and vitality as we age, and increase power on the bike.

The lower back, often referred to as the lumbar region, bears a tremendous burden as our bodies engage in daily activities and endure the wear and tear of life's demands. Unfortunately, this area is susceptible to breaking down and weakness leading to mobility decline, chronic pain, and even injury as we age... at least that is what we have been told.

This is just not true.

It's not age that leads to our lower backs hurting, loss of movement, or injury.

The real culprit is our never having been taught how to best move in ways that help bolster our backs health and abilities.

However, through better understanding of how the lower back and hips need to function, alongside having a targeted and intelligent strength training program to help reinforce spine-friendly movement patterns and improve strength-endurance, we can reverse this trend and forge a path towards resilience and longevity.

One of the primary benefits of strength training for the lower back lies in its ability to enhance muscular strength and stability.

The muscles surrounding the lower back, such as the erector spinae, multifidus, and quadratus lumborum, have long been thought to play a crucial role in maintaining posture and supporting the spine. However, as research has shown over the last 30+ years, this is, in fact, a mistake!

In reality, there is not a singular *"most important"* muscle when it comes to creating and supporting a healthy and pain-free lower back and hip area. Rather, ALL the muscles of the torso need to be fine-tuned to work together in chorus, in order to keep our spines healthy, happy, and pain free.

Much like a radio tower has guy wires to ensure that it stands strong and tall, so too with our spines!

As Dr. Stuart McGill explains in his exquisite book *Back Mechanic:*

"The first thing we need to establish is that the spine is not a freestanding pillar, such as Toronto's CN Tower or similar 'observation towers' found in Seattle and Auckland, floating among organs and flesh. Instead, we need to think of it more like a radio tower, those tall metallic structures stabilized by guy-wires that are connected to the ground. The function of these guy-wires is similar to that of the network of muscles and ligaments that surround our spinal columns: they provide strength and support. In the case of our backs, these 'anchoring' muscles also facilitate mobility. As with any part of our mobile bodies, from our elbows to our jaws, it is not our bones that create motion, but the muscles attached to them."

Strengthening the muscles through a training program that helps you learn how to better move provides the necessary support and stability, addressing issues related to poor posture and preventing breakdown of the tissues and structures. Learning how to move well helps bolster the spine's ability to start strong, resilient and injury free, while reducing the risk of chronic pain.

Moreover, intelligent strength training stimulates the growth and maintenance of healthy bone density. Aging naturally leads to bone loss, increasing the risk of osteoporosis and fractures. However, by incorporating exercises that target the lower back and hips, we can effectively slow down this process, helping our bones remain strong and resilient. Enhanced bone density not only contributes to a longer lifespan but also ensures that we lead an active and fulfilling life unencumbered by the fear of fractures.

What You Need to Know About Your Body & Heavy Lifting - If there's ANYTHING you take away from this book, let it be the following content...

When we strength train, we are putting a focused, specific stress on the body. Many of us think of strength training as targeting only the muscles, but in reality we need a few different things in our bodies to improve:

- The Bones

- The Nervous System

- The Muscle

- The Tendon

- The Fascia

- The Energy System

Each one of these systems has its own timeline, which it needs in order to actually adapt and get stronger. Having a basic understanding of each of these will help you get much better results from your strength training and allow you to better understand why consistent, year-round strength training is absolutely non-negotiable if you're serious about your health, longevity, and enjoyment of a quality life.

The Bones - Bones are an important part of our training, as they form the architecture that allows the fascia, muscles, and tendons to move us along.

Bone remodeling in the skeleton happens in 5 stages, and can take 4-8 months to complete. However, the bones of your spine, the vertebral bodies, are structures a bit different than the bones in your arms and legs, in that it comprises a scaffolding-like structure called *"trabeculae."*

These trabeculae fracture when placed under load, and take around 5 days to heal, thus bolstering their ability to resist force and not break. This is one of the many reasons that seasoned power lifters will not squat heavy or deadlift heavy within a 5-day period: They know that the spine and other tissues need time to recover and adapt!

This is one of the main reasons why I do not have athletes squat and deadlift heavy in the same session, or within the same 5 day period. We, as cyclists, where our spines are flexed forward for long periods of time without load, are especially susceptible to overloading the tissues of the spine, leading us to an injury or pain which was easily avoidable.

While many cyclists say they are strength training to improve bone health, what is missed is that in order for bone density and health to be improved, one must load them appropriately *year-round*. This has been shown by a number of researchers over the decades, yet the vast majority of endurance athletes fail to understand this.

Failure to stimulate the bones to adapt to a stimulus, means you lose the desired results.

Mark one down for year-round strength training!

The Nervous System - Perhaps one of the quickest to respond to a training stimulus, the nervous system is currently thought to take between 2-4 weeks to begin to adapt to a training stimulus (Journal of Applied Physiology, August 2021). In order to build to true peak-performances, the nervous system needs repeated exposures over time.

Strike another plus for year-round strength training!

Depending on the intensity and how hard you push, the nervous system can recover anywhere from 24-72 hours. However, lack of quality sleep and nutrition can significantly affect this timeframe.

The Muscle - Current understanding suggests that it takes the muscles between 4-8 weeks to adapt to a strength training stimulus. Once you remove that stimulus, the muscles will begin to lose these abilities.

Strike another one for year-round strength training!

But, it only takes 1-3 days for the muscles to recover from a workout, depending on how intense and difficult the training was. This is exactly why we recommend 2-3 strength training sessions a week- it's a balance of enough time between sessions that you can recover.

Tendons - Take around 48 hours to *begin* to adapt to training stimulus, but can take months to stiffen to a point where tendon health & performance are improved.

While tendons begin to respond relatively quickly, they also lose their abilities fairly quickly!

A study published in the Journal of Physiology in September 2007 led by

Maarten de Boer found significant breakdown in a tendon's mechanical abilities in just 2 weeks.

However, as noted above, tendons can take months to build up strength, and need regular stimulation (i.e. strength training) in order to improve.

Put another mark down for the necessity of <u>year-round</u> strength training! (I hope you've caught on to the theme here!)

The Fascia - Not yet really talked about in the mainstream media quite yet, the fascia has a huge impact on our movement and abilities. While we are still learning about this fascinating tissue, it is widely accepted that it takes the fascia 6-24 months to adapt to a training stimulus.

We currently do not fully understand the recovery timeline for fascia between training sessions, in part because this tissue is just now coming to the attention of researchers, and in part because it must be studied invivo. For now, this remains to be seen, but best current practices seem to suggest fascia-oriented training sessions can occur with quality every 2-7 days, depending on the individual.

In order to continue to build a better, more resilient and able fascia, you must continually stimulate it...

You guessed it, another strike for year-round strength training!

The Energy Systems - Localized energy systems (Metabolic Training, AKA "MetCons") can be a very useful part of a strength training program. However, because your primary sport of cycling is already a *"metabolic"* focused training program, we do need to be very careful that any metabolic work is focused in to your specific needs, and does not disrupt or interfere with the in-sport training program.

This is partially why in-season strength training should be *"heavy"* lifting, for fewer sets and repetitions: The longer the sets are (over 8 repetitions), the more the aerobic energy system needs to work. This means you're adding more training stress to your already "worked" energy system.

Metabolic training recovery will depend on the muscles or movements focused on, intensity, volume, and much more. Adaptations and recovery times will vary significantly depending on the individual.

"Use it or lose it!" applies here, and you guessed it...

Yet another strike for year-round strength training!

Life Pushes You Around

Alongside *"Use it or lose it"* there is a bigger thing that we need to think about:

Your Posture.

In this case it is not *"use it or lose it,"* but instead, it's the need to understand that hitting the weights and *"lifting heavy stuff!"* is not going to serve you very well, unless you can get yourself into better postures first. Otherwise, it is like putting a band-aid on a massive wound. Except in the case of lifting heavy stuff, you can do a lot more damage to yourself, and decrease your ability to stay active, healthy, and strong for many decades to come.

Our posture, or how we hold ourselves throughout our day-to-day lives, has a huge impact and influence on how we move and even on your ability to get into a recovery/ adaptation state. You see, for most people, as we age, our center of gravity gets pushed forward. Our head moves forward, our shoulders get pulled forward, and our hips get pushed forward. This is in part due to the fact we are constantly walking or moving forward throughout our days, as well as the fact that modern living has us sitting far more than ever before; especially in front of screens, where we bow our heads, or let our head and shoulders fall forward

Add on top of this riding a bike for 6+ hours a week where you are sitting in a crouched or rounded forward position for hours on end, and we have a recipe for things to get really out of alignment. This leads to things in our bodies changing roles, and even slacking off completely. From muscles on your backside getting stretched and hanging on for dear life, to the muscles on the front becoming short, stubborn, and seemingly impossible to move, the changes the body makes to muscles, fascia, and tissues is extensive.

The body will adapt to whatever activities we are doing consistently, in an effort to make it possible for us to perform these activities with as little effort as possible. So, if we are constantly in a set position for long periods of time, trying to accomplish some kind of work, whether riding a bike up a big mountain, or tapping away on our keyboards, the body will adjust to these demands to help the muscles do these tasks.

To put it simply:

Joint Position Dictates Muscle Function

Some mistakenly think that these adaptations for cycling are a good thing…*"Hey! This means I'll be super aero on the bike!"* Sure, that's one way to look at it.

But are you being paid mucho dinero to ride your bike each and every year?

I highly doubt it.

Even if you were being paid to ride your bike, we'd still want and need to get you into better postures and positions off the bike, so that your career will be longer, and you can perform at the highest level for many years.

When you have good posture and your joints are in positions as they are designed to work, there is less wear and tear on the system. This allows you far better performances as the body can perform the work and recover from it.

From muscles being able to work as they are meant to, as well as the fascia moving more freely and being able to transfer force and movements more easily, improving your posture has a massively positive trickle-down effect on everything you do throughout your day.

Perhaps one of the most overlooked, or not even thought of benefits of good posture, is the ability to rotate. Yes, really, the ability to rotate & turn around is greatly decreased as our center of gravity pulls us forward.

You can feel it yourself with this easy little test:

Stand up, put your feet shoulder width apart. Lean forward from your ankles, keeping your feet flat on the ground, and try to rotate your shoulders backwards as if looking behind you to each side.

Now stand tall and try it again.

Pretty cool, right?

Now here's the thing. If we can improve your posture and bring your center of gravity back to that when you are standing tall, your ears, shoulders, hips, knees, and ankles all align, amazing things will happen for you. Both on the bike and in your day-to-day life.

Learn How to Move Like an Athlete

Lifting things up and putting them down may be a nice general health goal, and indeed something which can help most people improve their overall well-being. But if you're a cyclist, just going into the weight room and lifting things with a goal of more weight or repetitions each week doesn't cut it.

Spending hours on our bikes in the riding position may be something we enjoy, but as with any sport, it takes a toll on the body.

Yes, we do want and need some adaptations to the riding position. But because we are not professionals who are being paid rather well to ride, it should be our main focus to keep the body healthy and in good working order. This is where learning to move well and working on things that help balance out the hours spent bent over the handlebars, can pay massive dividends.

"Everyone wants to look like an athlete or move like one... but nobody wants to train like one."

-Mark Reifkind

Intelligent strength training also places a strong emphasis on improving flexibility and joint mobility, specifically in the thoracic spine (upper back) and hips. Incorporating exercises that enhance range of motion and reduce stiffness in these areas allows for improved movement patterns. Enhanced flexibility, with strength and control through that new range of motion, not only reduces the risk of injury during physical activities, but also fosters an overall sense of ease and freedom of movement in daily life.

Additionally, targeting the lower back and hips in strength training helps to ease common issues associated with aging. As we age, the risk of developing degenerative conditions such as arthritis increases. By strengthening the muscles surrounding the spine and hips, we can enhance joint stability and reduce the strain on these areas, thereby minimizing the risk of developing degenerative conditions and preserving joint health.

Furthermore, strengthening the spine and hips contributes to the prevention and management of chronic pain. Lower back pain is a common complaint among individuals of all ages, but it becomes increasingly prevalent as we grow older. Engaging in intelligent strength training exercises specifically designed to target these areas and to teach better movement patterns can improve muscular endurance, reduce muscle imbalances, and promote proper alignment. This, in turn, alleviates pain and improves functional movement, allowing individuals to lead active and pain-free lives.

An often underestimated benefit of strength training lies in its ability to influence hormonal responses within our bodies. By engaging in regular strength training, we trigger the release of growth hormones, such as testosterone and human growth hormone itself. These hormones play crucial roles in muscle growth and repair, which, in turn, contribute to a stronger and more resilient body. They help to regenerate damaged tissues, reduce inflammation, and improve overall recovery. Additionally, increased muscle mass leads to a higher metabolic rate, making weight management more manageable and reducing the risk of chronic diseases such as obesity and diabetes. These factors collectively promote a longer and healthier life.

Recognizing the science behind ageless strength is instrumental in adopting a holistic approach to strength training. By understanding the physiological benefits of intelligent strength training and specifically targeting the spinal column and hips to work more as designed, we unlock the key to longevity. Strengthening the muscles in these areas provides support and stability, promoting proper posture, improving breathing patterns, and reducing chronic pain. Improving bone density reduces the risk of osteoporosis and fractures, ensuring a resilient skeletal structure. Hormonal responses triggered by strength training aid in muscle growth, repair, and weight management, supporting a longer and healthier life. Enhanced flexibility and joint mobility, when built with appropriate strength and control through the newly gained ranges of motion, can significantly reduce the risk of injury, improve movement patterns, and preserve joint health, contributing to a vibrant and active lifestyle. Furthermore, building strength in the hips and midsection to properly support the lower back and deflect forces around the spine and instead through the hips and shoulders, helps prevent and manage common age-related issues such as degenerative conditions and chronic pain.

May we all embark on this journey together, harnessing the power of ageless strength to nurture and preserve our bodies, ultimately unlocking the extraordinary potential to live a vibrant, fulfilling, and prolonged life.

Chapter Three

Where Are You Now?

Assessing Your Strength & Mobility

Understanding your current strength levels and establishing a baseline for targeted improvement.

Assessing your strength and mobility is a crucial first step in any fitness journey. It not only provides you with a clear understanding of your current abilities, but also helps you identify areas that require improvement for optimal performance.

Strength is the foundation of any physical activity, whether it's lifting weights, running, or participating in sports. It encompasses both muscular strength, which is the force that your muscles can generate, and functional strength, which is the ability to use that strength during everyday activities. To accurately assess your strength, you need to consider various factors and conduct a range of exercises that target different muscle groups.

A simple method that many personal trainers and coaches look to use for assessing your strength is by performing basic strength tests such as push-ups, pull-ups, squats, and planks.

However, over my nearly 20 years working with cyclists (and triathletes) of all ages, these tests often leave one feeling more beat up and sore, than proving useful... that is unless you have already been strength training for some time.

So what I've presented here is a different assessment:

One where we look at movement qualities.

This approach allows you to more quickly understand where you are, which allows you to move more quickly towards lifting heavy stuff in a safe, targeted manner.

These assessment movements target major muscle groups and can be easily measured to track progress over time. By recording the number of repetitions or duration of each exercise, you can establish a baseline for improvement.

For the push-up test, start by performing as many full push-ups as you can with proper form. If you cannot do a full push-up, modify it by doing knee push-ups or using an elevated surface. Push-ups primarily target the chest, shoulders, and triceps, but they also engage the core and upper back muscles.

The pull-up test evaluates your upper body pulling strength. Hang from a bar with an overhand grip and try to pull your chin above the bar as many times as you can. If you cannot do a full pull-up, use bands or assistive machines to gradually build your strength. Pull-ups primarily target the back, biceps, and grip strength.

Lower body strength can be assessed through exercises like squats and lunges. Squats can be performed with bodyweight only or with additional weight such as a barbell or dumbbells. Focus on reaching at least parallel depth with proper form while maintaining stable knees and a neutral spine. Lunges, on the other hand, challenge your leg strength and balance. Pay attention to maintaining proper knee alignment and control throughout the movement.

Movement Assessment:

- Hands Overhead squat (FMS)

- Seated Rotation

- Single leg supported Romanian Deadlift

- Standing Rotation

- Behind the back Shoulder Reach

- Goblet Squat

- Kettlebell Deadlift not to floor

- Pushups

I have video examples/demonstrations of the above exercises that you can access for free at https://www.youtube.com/playlist?list=PL2scKg9aZ87wh67bRZ 49KgQFvMnAb7M5C .

To assess your mobility, you must consider the range of motion in your joints and muscles. Mobility is essential not only for proper functioning but also for injury prevention. Limited mobility can lead to imbalances, compensations, and limitations in overall performance.

One effective method for assessing mobility is through specific movement tests. These tests evaluate the flexibility and range of motion in different areas of your body. For example, the deep squat test requires you to perform a full-depth squat with proper form, assessing the mobility of your ankles, knees, hips, and lower back. Another test is the shoulder mobility test, which evaluates the flexibility and range of motion in your shoulders.

For the deep squat test, start by assuming a shoulder-width stance and squat as low as you can while keeping your heels on the ground and maintaining proper form. Ensure that your knees track over your toes and your chest stays upright. If you struggle to perform a full-depth squat, it may indicate limited ankle mobility or tightness in your hips or lower back.

The shoulder mobility test involves reaching one arm overhead and behind your back, attempting to touch the opposite shoulder blade. Switch sides and repeat. This test assesses the flexibility and mobility in your shoulder joints, which is crucial for various upper body movements.

In addition to these basic strength and mobility tests, it is advisable to consult with a qualified fitness professional or physical therapist. They can provide more detailed assessments and identify any specific limitations or imbalances that need to be addressed.

Once you have completed these assessments, you can develop a targeted training plan that focuses on improving your weaknesses and building upon your strengths. This plan should include exercises and techniques that address your specific needs. For example, if you have identified weak glutes, incorporating exercises like hip thrusts or glute bridges can help strengthen these muscles.

Regular reassessments are essential to track progress and adjust your training as needed. Repeating the same strength and mobility tests every few weeks or months will help you gauge improvement and identify areas that still require attention.

Remember, assessing your strength and mobility is not about comparing yourself to others or striving for perfection. It is about understanding where you are starting from and setting realistic goals for improvement. With a solid foundation of knowledge about your current abilities, you can confidently embark on your fitness journey and work towards reaching your full potential.

In the next chapter, we will delve into the importance of lifting smart and lifting heavy to maximize your strength gains. Stay tuned!

Chapter Four

Lift Smart, Lift Heavy

In this chapter, we will delve deeper into the art of lifting smart and lifting heavy. We will explore strategic approaches to lifting heavy weights that enhance performance without compromising joint health.

Exploring Strategic Approaches

When it comes to lifting heavy weights, it is essential to approach it strategically in order to optimize performance while safeguarding your joints. By implementing the following strategies, you can take your lifting to the next level:

Periodization

Periodization is a systematic approach to training that involves dividing your training into specific phases or cycles. This approach allows you to vary the intensity, volume, and exercises performed during different periods, providing your body with adequate time to recover and adapt. By utilizing periodization, you can optimize your gains while minimizing the risk of overuse injuries.

There are many different types of periodization models, such as linear periodization and undulating periodization. Linear periodization involves gradually increasing the intensity and lowering the volume as you progress through training cycles. This method is most often used by self-coached athletes preparing for specific events or competitions, as it is fairly easy to understand and plan. It is also the way many new coaches are taught how to plan and program, as it is fairly easy to teach.

On the other hand, undulating periodization involves varying the intensity and volume within each training cycle. This approach is typically used by individuals who aim to continuously change their training in an effort to keep from getting bored, or to change how hard they are pushing month to month.

These are just two examples of the well over 20 different periodization approaches that one can use. The most important point is that in order to see improvements, you'll need to have a program and a plan that allows you to systematically increase the challenge to the body, but that also plans recovery periods in order to allow you to not only adapt and improve, but to also stay healthy.

Load Management

Proper load management is crucial for lifting heavy weights without compromising joint, bone, and tissue health. It involves manipulating the weight, sets, and repetitions to optimize performance and prevent overuse injuries. It's important to strike the right balance between challenging your muscles and allowing sufficient recovery.

Using a load that is too heavy for your current technique level and strength level can lead to improper form, which increases stress on your joints, bones and connective tissues. On the other hand, using a load that is too light may not provide the necessary stimulus for muscle growth and strength gains. Gradually increasing the load over time while maintaining good form is key to lifting heavy smartly and safely. However, as an endurance athlete, and someone wanting to stay strong, healthy, and able-bodied for many years to come, your technique for a movement will be your guide as to how much you can (or should) load a movement.

This is one of the biggest "secrets" that the top power lifters and Olympic weight lifters know:

In order to move heavy, you first must move well.

Through every set, every repetition, and every strength training session, the focus must always be on how you are moving, letting technique guide your weight selection for that day, and that exercise... **Not** what you did last week, or a month ago.

This is where learning to strength train off of Rate of Perceived Exertion (RPE) or Repetitions in Reserve (RIR) allows you to see better, more consistent progress, and performance improvements that stick.

Training By RPE or RIR

Have you ever gone out for a ride, and on that ride you feel (and see) that you're climbing faster, yet it feels easier than usual?

And what about those days on the other side of things- you're climbing slower and it feels way harder?

Same climb, different "readiness" in your body.

While we have been led to believe that fitness & health improvements come in a straight line up. This could not be any further from the truth.

Our body's readiness to perform a given task will change day to day, depending on a number of things:

- How much you slept

- How well you slept

- Hydration status

- If you've eaten enough

- If you've eaten enough of the things your body needs

- Your life stress

- The accumulated training stress from that past few days & weeks

- Your mental state

Just to name a few!

This is one of the biggest tripping blocks on the way to improved strength and fitness.

But there is a simple, technology-free way that you can better meet your body and it's abilities on that day:

Train by FEEL.

I know, I know, what about all this technology, and your "recovery score", etc.?!?

Well, these things are trying to put a number on something we each can actually feel, so long as we learn to tune in to our bodies.

RPE (Rate of Perceived Exertion) or RIR (Repetitions in Reserve) is extremely easy and useful in helping you get it right.

In fact, in a convergent study done in 2022 at Canterbury Christ Church University in Kent, United Kingdom (PMID: 35000021), they looked at over 110 different research studies that looked at whether RPE was as good as physical indicators (Heart Rate, Blood Pressure, Blood Lactic Acid, etc) in determining physical strain, and found that it was just as good!

What is RPE?

RPE (Rate of Perceived Exertion) is simply asking "On a scale of 1-10 how hard was the exercise?"

1= light as a feather

10= Maximum effort, I have nothing left

RPE CHART

RPE	FEELS LIKE
10	MAX EFFORT
9	1 GOOD REP LEFT
8	2 GOOD REPS LEFT
7	3-4 GOOD REPS LEFT
6	4+ GOOD REPS LEFT
0-5	WARMUP / EASY

As noted above, we must let technique drive our strength training, in order to allow us to continue to gain strength, get the intended improvements we want, and to stay healthy. So we simply add to the end "With great technique".

What is RIR?

RIR (Repetitions in Reserve) is essentially another way to look at RPE, with a bit more refinement.

RIR looks at "how many repetitions left do I think I have?".

Again here, we have to add "with great technique".

So a RIR 1= you have ONE Repetition with great technique left.

An RIR 3 = you have Three repetitions with great technique left.

The genius of these two systems is that they allow you to not only focus on keeping great technique, but also shift the focus on where you are on that day, at that time. This leave the weight you choose to matter only in that it meets the necessary RPE or RIR for that day.

This allows you to dial down or up your load (weight on the bar), to meet your body exactly where it is on that day, at that time. IF you want to lift heavy or see performance improvements in your riding - and especially if you want both- there is no other way than to use RPE or RIR to guide your weight selection each workout and each set.

Lift "Heavy," Smarter

With research these days touting the benefits of heavy training for cyclists and triathletes, we've seen a bit of a rush to **"Lift Heavy $h*t."** Unfortunately, what many fail to realize, including myself in the first few years of my coaching practice, is that the research is ***easily 5-10 years behind*** what is being done at the leading edge of training and sports performance. I'd argue in the case of strength training for cycling and triathlon, that we are closer to 10-15 years behind, in this specific area.

I am not saying this to bash or berate the researchers who are doing a lot of hard work to discover the mechanisms and reasons behind what we do. Rather, I want you to better understand where the articles, content, and hot topics are coming from, and what they may actually offer you in your quest to health, strength, and fitness.

The way many of us, as beginners, think of as "heavy" is a bigger weight.

More kilos or pounds on our back or in our hands.

While this is certainly the most easy way to look at "heavy," it actually does very little in the way of building better performances and abilities for you. As someone seeking to have more longevity and life in your years ahead, we want to go a few layers deeper.

Believe it or not, even the strongest women and men in the world do not go based on the weight on the bar for their day in and day out sessions.

They go by _how_ it feels to them.

They follow the RPE or RIR approaches we spoke about earlier. This is not to say they do not program for a specific percentage of their estimated

One Repetition Maximum (1RM). But rather, they will work at far lighter weights, focusing on technique and bar speed (also called Velocity Based Training, or VBT), and the Quality of their Training time.

One of the All-Time greats of Olympic lifting, Multi-Olympic Champion Tommy Kono shared a great gem in his book *Weightlifting, Olympic Style*:

"Many lifters (and coaches, as well) feel...that since heavy weights handled in training will increase your strength that heavier weights will develop strength even quicker.

How wrong they can be in thinking this way. In many instances, a longer time spent in the gym can retard your progress and using extremely heavy weights can ruin your coordination, reflex, timing, and technique."

While Tommy is talking specifically about Olympic lifting (thus the coordination, reflex, and timing), he is correct about too much time in the gym retarding your progress.

If you spend too much energy in the gym trying to lift really heavy things, you will need to pay the price in terms of time and energy for adaptations to happen, and for you to recover.

This is where it is absolutely integral, if not vital, to keep in mind that dead lifting or squatting more weight does NOT necessarily mean more power or better performances on the bike!

Yes, current research at the time of publishing this book in 2024 is showing improvements in power after "lifting heavy," however what the researchers have not yet explored is the why behind it. And that is primarily neurological changes to the neuromuscular system.

More of the neuromuscular system is being recruited.

These studies have been very helpful in getting folks to move towards the strength training they need, but have yet to explore the long-term necessities of improvement in timing, tissue qualities, movement and tensioning of the fascia, and a host of other improvements that must be made through purposeful and focused practices of strength training.

So while simply picking up a bigger, heavier weight may seem like the end-all be-all, it is very far from it... especially if you want to look, move, and feel great for the next 15, 20, 30+ years.

True Sport Specificity

Let's take a quick dive into the considerations you must take into account before lifting heavy stuff, as well as sport-specific considerations: The REAL sport specific considerations, not the "doing an exercise that looks like my sport, so that must be sport specific" mindset.

As we discussed in Chapter 2, the positions and postures that you need to hold on the bike tend to speed up the process of our center of gravity to be pushed forward. This leads to joints being out of positions that allow them to perform well, as well as more wear and tear to be placed on the system, and your recovery and adaptation times to be longer.

In each and every sport, there is a set of physical and mental skills that need to be developed. It is extremely tempting to simply look for movements in your strength training that look very similar to what you do in sport, and then label them as sport specific. However, there are a few more, much deeper, ways in which we want to assess your sport in order to build a truly specific demand-oriented training program.

- Postures & positions required

- Energy Systems

- Type of strength needed

These three items will primarily drive our sport-specific strength program, but not necessarily in a way that many think.

Looking at postures and positions we want to understand how these each affect the body's ability to perform well:

- What kinds of forces are being placed on the body?

- How are repetitive movements affecting the person?

- What kinds of tissues and joints are being compromised by the sport?

From there, the strength training program will be designed to help build proximal stiffness (everything between your neck, elbows, and knees) to give you better movement distally (from the shoulders and hips).

Looking at the Energy Systems, we want to understand:

- What are the primary energy systems for this sport?

- What energy systems are not challenged as much?

- What is needed to help drive better recovery between efforts?

Last, we'll want to determine what kind of strength is needed:

- Is it a high torque?

- Explosive, singular efforts (such as pole vaulting, shot put)?

- Pulsing (such as running and biking)?

- Is it high force (i.e. rugby, American football)?

Applying the Sport Specificity to Cyclists

Of course, there are other considerations as well, including injury history, previous training experiences, lifestyle, goals, to name a few. However, the sport specificity, while it takes into consideration the highly repetitive movements, does NOT mean copying the movements in your strength training!

In fact, one of the best things we can do, is help teach your body how to balance out these highly repetitive movements through your strength training, looking to compliment these postures, positions, and movements, by working to regain lost ranges of motion by adding appropriate strength, regaining tissue qualities, and building back the abilities often lost due to playing or performing in your sport.

That said, there are times, especially for professionals- those earning money to compete- where we allow for more sport positional adaptations to be a bit out of balance. Such as a Grande Tour rider who is undertaking one of the biggest feats of human endurance in simply completing that monumental race.

However, the reason we allow those changes to go is not to get better performance, but instead because of the amount of energy needed in order to keep the rider moving down the road. There simply is not enough energy for the body to both complete 21 days of burning well north of 5,000 calories in their event, and to have the energy available to sufficiently support the baseline bodily functions (energetically often labeled as "Resting Metabolic Rate").

As masters riders who are looking to enjoy our riding, running, and swimming for many years to come, and more often than not looking to increase our longevity and health, it is absolutely vital that we begin looking at "sport specificity" as laid out above, and begin to think *"How do I stack the cards in my favor? What am I not getting in my riding movements, and how can I regain great posture and improve my ability to keep my muscles, tissues, and joints healthy and feeling great?"*

This question can be answered in part, by learning how to lift heavy things, but in a way that helps counterbalance the in-sport demands, and to give you the tissue, movements, and postures that you don't get in cycling. . . but the key here is not to just "Lift heavy $h*t", it is to do it in a way that is sustainable, and will help you stay healthy, get stronger, and move better.

How to Lift Heavy Stuff, Sustainably

As we spoke about a bit earlier in this chapter, RPE and RIR are going to be much better measures for you on a day-to-day basis of what "heavy" is to your body each day. These would be the all-important foundations that you must learn first, as they allow you to build a wonderful tower of health, fitness, and performance upon them.

But what can, or should, you progress to once RPE and RIR have become a well-developed skill for you?

Here are a few more advanced ways to continue to develop your abilities to lift heavy things, without leaving your mind and body smashed to bits.

Ladder Sets

Ladder sets are a wonderful training tool, when used appropriately. In its basic form, a ladder set is simply sets which move in ascending or descending number of repetitions per set. Within each set we can either keep the RPE or RIR the same, or change it to match the desired outcome.

Over my career working with professional basketball players and endurance athletes, ladder sets have proven to be incredibly valuable, as we can easily get higher intensity lifts (using more weight, consistent velocities) while decreasing the overall volume (total weight moved) in a strength session. This allows you to get exactly what you need, without taking a huge toll on the tissues or nervous system.

An example of a ladder scheme I've used with great success is 8, 5, 3, with each set targeting an RPE 7, we're able to get *"heavy"* lifting in, without completely smashing you to bits. The RPE of 7 allows the heavy weights to be moved with much better technique, and focus on intent.

Of course, as you move through the hypertrophy and max strength stages of the training year those RPE's will change, up to an 8 or even possibly 9, but it is all dependent on what your needs are from your strength training, how well you're recovering and adapting to your riding, and what will give you the most return on your effort and energies.

Sometimes it is heavier weights, other times it is showing up and doing just enough work to get the adaptations you need from that training.

Tempo Training

Tempo training involves manipulating the speed at which you perform each repetition. By changing the speed of each specific, you can not only change the intensity and difficulty of the exercise, but also the outcome of the results you'll gain from performing it in that fashion.

Tempo training techniques include tempo contrast training, where you alternate between slow and explosive movements in the same exercise, and isometric pauses, where you hold a specific position for up to a few seconds during the movement.

When performing tempo based movements written into a training program, they (tempo) can apply to a wide variety of exercises, from squats and deadlifts, to bicep curls and leg extensions. Changing the tempo of an exercise can be an incredibly powerful tool when used well.

There are 2 different ways to write Tempo into training programs, both are correct.

Some coaches use a 4 number sequence, as follows:

1 - 2 - 3 - 4

While others use a 3 number sequence, as follows:

1 - 2 - 3

The 1st number is ALWAYS the eccentric portion of the movement, or the lengthening of the main working muscle. So for Squats, and bench press, it is the lowering of the weight. Pretty easy, right?

Well, for deadlifts and pull-ups or lat pull-downs, it can be a bit confusing, as for deadlifts this number is the lowering of the weight from the *"standing tall"* position.

And for the pull-ups, it is the lowering of the body from the top position, while for the lat pull-downs it is the bar moving upwards from the chest.

The 2nd number is the end of the eccentric movement.

This number notes a pause, or isometric hold, before you begin the concentric part of the exercise.

For the squat, it's the bottom of your squat, where you are able to keep spine-neutral, with your feet flat, and tension through the glutes. While for the Deadlift, it is when the weight is just above the floor, hovering (or on the floor).

The 3rd number is the concentric movement, or shortening of the main working muscle.

For squats, it is the standing portion, and the same for deadlifts and bench press.

The 4th number, which not all coaches use, is the *"pause"* or *"reset"* at the beginning point of an exercise, such as standing tall with the barbell for a squat or deadlift, or holding the bar at arm's length for the bench press.

Before I started mainly coaching cyclists and triathletes in strength training in 2007, I used a 3 number system. This is because many of the people I was coaching were basketball players and ball sport athletes (i.e. Soccer, Racquetball/ Squash, and Softball). For those folks, it was rare to have someone who needed to learn how to better stand with no tension in their bodies, as many of their sports rewarded great posture.

But with cyclists and triathletes, who spend a lot of time on the bike, there was an enormous reward to learning this skill, and how to appropriately hold a great standing position. So we use the 4 number system here at Human Vortex Training LLC.

A few important points about tempo training are:

- Slowing down the eccentric (lengthening of the prime mover muscle) phase of the movement can increase time under tension and induce greater muscle activation. But this approach also creates more tissue damage, which makes it a generally poor choice for use during your primary riding season/race season.

- Adding in an isometric pause or hold under tension can allow you to improve connective tissue strength, learn how to create force from different pathways from that position, as well as help you tune-in to better, more advantageous movement patterns.

- In the early season, after you've done some slower tempo and isometric pause training, and you're looking to stack the cards in your favor to turn your weight room strength into on-bike performances, adding an explosive ("X") component to the concentric movement can help you build the skill of keeping proximal stiffness, to get distal performance and power.

- Or put more simply: You learn how to create and control power, so you're not "firing a cannon from a canoe".

- Using tempo as a technique within your strength training

programming can enhance performance, improve muscle control, increase performance benefits, and even reduce joint stress. In fact, a form of tempo lifting has even been used in cardiac rehab clinics, under the watchful eye of Cardiac Rehabilitation Specialists, to help those with certain heart ailments, to improve strength, circulation, and all-around health.

There are several way to incorporate a tempo training scheme, such as a 3-1-3-1 tempo (3 seconds on the eccentric phase, 1 second pause, and 3 second concentric phase, 1 second to reset), which we use here at Human Vortex Training LLC. to either help those new to a specific movement to learn how to execute it properly, or to allow our athletes who are traveling and who may not have access to the weights they need to get a better training effect from what they do have available.

Needless to say, it can be a valuable tool in your heavy lifting arsenal and should not be overlooked.

Cluster Sets

Cluster sets, on the other hand, involve breaking down a heavy set into smaller, more manageable clusters with short rest periods in-between. This allows you to lift a heavier load overall while maintaining good form and minimizing the stress on your joints. For example, instead of performing one set of eight repetitions with a heavy weight, you can perform two sets of four repetitions with a short rest period (e.g., 20-30 seconds) in-between, where you re-rack the weight during the mini rest period.

This is a great tool for those who find that heavy strength training often leaves them extremely sore for a few days after, or for those looking to build their resiliency and strength while keeping great technique throughout.

Velocity Based Training

Perhaps the least well-known until recently, due in large part to the expensive equipment necessary (starting around $2,000USD in early 2000s), Velocity Based Training has worked its way out of high-level training facilities, and down to commercial and small, locally owned gyms, thanks to advances in technology and lower production costs.

That said, Velocity Based Training, when done by a strength training athlete who is experienced, has taken the time to build sound movement patterns for the movements, and who understands how to appropriately execute it, can be very beneficial.

This approach to training allows you low "heavy" in a way that allows you to produce high-power for a given movement (like a Hex Bar (Trap Bar) Deadlift, Front Squat, Back Squat, or Goblet Squat), allowing you to hone in on movement challenges, power delivery challenges, or the desired specific outcomes.

But let me make this crystal clear: <u>Velocity Based Training is a more advanced strength training tool, and it is absolutely not appropriate for those new to strength training, and/or those who are still working to be able to execute the given movement with sound technique.</u>

If you do not have great technique under loads towards an RPE 8-9 in any given rep range, or if you find towards the end of your sets that your technique is becoming significantly worse... Velocity Based Training is not (yet) for you.

For those who have put in the 4+ years of consistent work on their main lifts, Barbell/Hex bar based, to become technically sound, and who are looking to dive into velocity based training, there are a few things you'll need to know:

To paraphrase Anatoliy Bondarchuk:

There is a proper order of training for adaptations to occur. Fail to keep this order, and you'll lose the adaptations twice over: First, because the individual wasn't properly prepared to train properly for that manner (along the lines of throwing a Ferrari engine into the frame of a '79 Pinto), and Second, there will not be as significant increase in performance when or if the athlete is finally prepared for it, since that particular training stimulus was already used and adapted to.

There is an order of operations.

Fail to follow it, and you'll lose out twice (and open yourself up to a higher risk of injury).

If you want to begin to become more aware of the velocities you use in your training, and begin to learn about VBT, you have two options, really:

1. Find a reputable coach with experience in coaching and programming VBT programs.

2. Learn on your own as you go.

Let's talk a few details about Velocity Based Training, as the foundations you need to have before using it, or even thinking about using it, are the very same that every single masters cyclist will need.

Level 1- Foundation: Movement proficiency, Mobility, and Resiliency

As mentioned above, before even considering using velocity based training, you will need to have rock solid basics.

For masters cyclists, this will mean your Barbell Squat (Front or Back, whatever you choose), and Hex Bar Deadlift or Romanian Deadlift techniques should be solid.

For those who either have had higher level weight room training, perhaps from playing a sport in college, or who have found enjoyment in CrossFit, or who want to explore the world of Olympic Lifting, High Hang Cleans will also be a staple in your programming.

For those who do not have an Olympic Weightlifting background, or who do not want to put the time or effort into learning them, Kettlebell swings are a nice stand in. However, to my knowledge, there are no parameters for VBT with the kettlebell swings.

Along with these main lifts being extremely clean and well practiced, you'll also want to have the appropriate mobility to be able to move through these movements properly.

Note that does not mean you need to squat *"ass to grass"* or to deadlift off the floor. It does mean that you should have trained these movements enough over the years, that you have an excellent feel for the movements, and are able to appropriately gauge what you are able to do on a given day. And you can properly move through the required range of motion without compensations, such as a hip shift, a heel coming off the floor, or any other, to help you *"get around"* a mobility or strength through range of motion issue.

If you USED to be able to do a great barbell front squat to parallel with great technique... years ago... but now you lack the mobility and posture to do them... Velocity Based Training is not (yet) for you.

The other part of this foundational level is resiliency. Can you bounce back well from moderate to heavy strength training, on top of your riding? If it takes you 4 full days to not have any kind of soreness from your strength training, then we are nowhere near being ready for velocity based training.

Instead, you should choose one of the other routes to use, while putting your focus on improving your consistency with your nutrition, sleep, and stress management so you can better recover from your current training loads.

Level 2- Foundation: Base Strength

Before we can get to lifting heavy with velocity, there needs to be a baseline of strength.Once again, year-round strength will allow for the needed physical changes within the muscle to occur.

I tend to look for a baseline of having strength trained year-round for at least 2-3 consecutive years, with the individual being able to, on average, bounce back from a moderate intensity strength session (RPE 6-7 in whole) within 24 hours.

While you may be thinking base strength = weights one can move as compared to body weight (AKA 1 Rep Max), what I'm looking for is a strong and resilient athlete who has created the physical changes within the muscle to be able to handle the Challenges of VBT.

Level 3- Foundation: Max Strength

We cannot ignore Max Strength, as some kind of training at higher levels, learning what it means to be near one's limit IS important.

Velocity-Based Training requires you to be able to sense where you are, and how quickly things are moving towards your limits for that lift.

You need to be able to know when you're flying towards your limits, and cut it off before things get dangerous.

Velocity Training: Know Your Performance Specific Outcomes First

When you've properly built the foundation for it, VBT can be a powerful tool in helping you to dial in to your specific in-sport demands.

For example, if you're a track cyclist or CX mountain biker, do you need Starting Strength? If so, we'll be looking to move at 1.3m/s or faster for your deadlift or hang high clean.

But if you need more acceleration abilities, we'll be wanting 0.50- 0.75 m/s.

These are just a few basic examples here to help you understand that simply slapping a velocity measuring device into a bar and trying to *"move fast"* is not going to help you. There are a whole host of velocity ranges which exist that you'll need to be familiar with if you want to get what you need out of using VBT as a part of your training.

When (or more likely if) you are interested in learning about VBT training, Dr. Bryan Mann's *Developing Explosive Athletes: Use of Velocity Based Training in Training Athletes* is a great place to start.

Again, VBT is an advanced approach to training, and for the vast majority of masters cyclists who are looking to strength training to improve their cycling performance, it may not even be necessary, as mastering the basics we discuss throughout this book will give you the big returns you're in search of.

Prehabilitation Exercises

Prehabilitation exercises, also known as prehab exercises, are designed to help prevent injuries, enhance joint health, improve tissue qualities, and allow better breathing, posture, and movement. These exercises target the muscles and movements commonly neglected or beat-up by hours in the saddle, and those involved in heavy lifting, emphasizing stability, flexibility, and balance. These exercises are often geared towards *"target areas"* due to your movement preferences and/ or sport.

Including prehab exercises in your warm-up routine, or as *"filler"* exercises; Exercises added before or after the primary moves, can help activate the necessary muscles, improve joint mobility, and reinforce proper movement patterns. These Pre-hab exercises can help you address the *"big things"* over a long period, when they are included in your dynamic warm-up or programming.

Some prehab exercises that are often recommended for cyclists to improve their posture and movement include:

- **Breathwork:** Learning how to better move air in and out with each breath, not only helps you to breathe better, but it can also help mobilize tight joints, improve joint alignment, and even help tight muscles begin to free up! As an additional bonus, including breathwork at the beginning and end of your strength training helps to create a better internal environment that will help you perform better (at the start) and kick start the recovery process (at the end).

- **Thoracic Extension Exercises:** Your rib cage (Thorax) includes over 80 different joints between your spine, ribs, and shoulders. These joints, and the muscles and tissues that run between them, often become tight on the front, and lengthened on the back, thanks to the long hours we spend on our bikes and sitting in our day-to-day lives. You can use breathing exercises, like the Active Preacher Stretch, to help regain some of the mobility and balance needed to live a healthier life and be able to handle the rigors of lifting heavy stuff.

- **Shoulder Blade Movement:** Many cyclists lose the ability to raise their hands up overhead, and to move freely from their shoulders. Learning to move your shoulder blades on the rib cage not only helps to decrease neck and shoulder pain, but also improves your ability to steer the bike, and can significantly improve your quality of life day to day.

- **Hip Strength & Mobility Exercises:** Incorporate exercises like focused glute work like clamshells, integrated glute work like hip airplanes, split squats or suitcase carries can help you improve hip strength, while targeted dynamic stretches and breathing exercises can help improve mobility and prevent imbalances.

- **Foot Strength & Ankle Mobility:** The foot and lower leg are often neglected in the cycling world, yet they play a huge role in your riding performance. Doing exercises for ankle mobility such as calf stretches, ankle circles, and ankle dorsiflexion exercises to improve range of motion and stability during lower body exercises like squats and deadlifts.

Choosing the best pre-hab exercises and understanding where to place them for best results is part art, and part skill. You can certainly put together your own pre-hab exercise list and dabble to find what works for you, however it is best to consult a qualified fitness professional to tailor prehab exercises specifically to your individual needs and weaknesses.

Recovery Strategies

Perhaps the largest obstacle for cyclists looking to strength train to overcome, is the ability to recover from your strength sessions, so you can ride with quality.

Lifting heavy weights places a considerable demand on your body's energy systems and tissues. Add to that the energy demands of riding, and it can seem like an impossible task to balance both. However, by having a plan that is thought out ahead of time, and implementing effective recovery strategies into that plan, is crucial to prevent overuse injuries, managing your energy, and optimizing your performance. Here are some key recovery practices to consider:

- **Breathwork:** Yup. Here we are again, talking about breathing. Using breathing at the end of each training session can help you kick start your recovery by changing your internal environment (hormonal). Taking 3-5 minutes to perform something like "box breathing" (5 sec inhale thru nose- 2 sec hold- 5 sec exhale mouth- 2 sec hold) is easy to incorporate.

- **Rest and Sleep:** Adequate rest and quality sleep are essential for muscle recovery and repair. Aim for 7-9 hours of uninterrupted sleep each night to support your body's rejuvenation process. Best practice is to have a regular bedtime +/- 15 minutes, and to stick to it.

- **Nutrition:** Proper nutrition plays a vital role in recovery. Consuming a balanced diet that includes an adequate amount of protein, carbohydrates, and fats is crucial for repairing damaged muscles and replenishing energy stores. Additionally, including foods rich in antioxidants, such as fruits and vegetables, can help reduce inflammation and aid in recovery.

- **Foam Rolling and Stretching:** Incorporating fascial massage, AKA foam rolling, and stretching exercises can help alleviate muscle tightness and improve joint mobility. Spend time targeting the specific muscles used during heavy lifting to release tension and aid in recovery. Foam rolling can be done before or after a workout, and static stretching should only be done as part of a cool-down routine.

- **Active Recovery:** Engaging in low-intensity activities, such as light cardio or yoga, on your rest days can promote blood circulation and muscle regeneration. Active recovery aids in flushing out metabolic waste and reducing post-workout soreness.

- **Recovery Modalities:** Utilizing recovery modalities such as cryotherapy, compression boots, sauna or steam room, or massage can provide additional benefits for reducing inflammation and enhancing recovery. However, these modalities should be used in conjunction with other recovery practices and under professional guidance.

- **Hydration:** Staying adequately hydrated is essential for optimal performance and recovery. Dehydration can impair fascia and muscle function, increase the risk of injuries, and delay the recovery process. Aim to drink water consistently throughout the day, both during and outside of your workouts. This is especially true in the colder periods of the year, when we are less likely to think about staying on top of our hydration.

- *"Leaving some on the table"* **at each strength training session:** While building fitness on the bike will lead us to times where we *"leave it all out there,"* strength training, especially if you're looking for better performance on the bike, or to lift heavy stuff, means that you actually want to finish each session with a little in the tank.

This is something I've heard over and over throughout my career from top athletes and coaches alike. From world-renowned low back specialist

Dr. Stuart McGill, to world-record holder for the squat (1,306 pounds, if you're wondering) Brian Carroll, to top Crossfit Athletes and pro basketball players... When it comes to their day-to-day strength training, they leave a little in the tank. Then, on Competition day, they go as hard as they need to in order to see success and play at the level needed.

Training to mechanical, or muscular, failure is a fool's errand; especially as we move into our 40s and beyond, and even more so as cyclists.

As we age, the body and its structures take longer to adapt to the stresses we've placed on it, recover from that training, and express it either as strength or fitness. And as endurance sports athletes or participants, we are already working our bodies' abilities to sustain activity for long periods of time, pushing the limits of the energy available to repair and improve.

In conclusion, lifting smart and lifting heavy can go hand in hand when you implement strategic approaches to optimize performance without compromising tissue or joint health. By incorporating periodization, managing loads, utilizing tempo training, including prehab exercises, and implementing effective recovery strategies, you can take your lifting to improve your cycling performances to new heights while avoiding injury. Remember, always prioritize proper form and technique, listen to your body, and gradually progress to ensure long-term success and enjoyment in your weightlifting journey.

Chapter Five

The Art of Recovery

In this chapter, we will delve even further into the art of recovery and explore a comprehensive range of techniques and practices that are essential for sustaining a robust strength training routine. Recovery is far too often overlooked or underestimated in the realm of fitness, but it is **THE** integral part of the equation for achieving optimal strength, performance, and overall well-being.

If you fail to give your body the appropriate time and energy availability needed to recover and adapt to a training stimulus, where on the bike or in strength, you are simply making yourself tired for zero gain or improvement.

"It is not the tenacity or intensity of a workout which gains you the results, it is the consistency over time, and ensuring you have enough time and energy between training sessions to allow the body to recover and adapt."

Unveiling Recovery Techniques and Practices

Let's unveil a range of recovery techniques and practices that are vital for your strength training routine:

The Importance of Recovery

It is crucial to understand why recovery is so important. When you engage in strength training, your muscles undergo microtrauma, causing inflammation, which brings blood and the nutrients necessary for repair and improvement to the area. This requires energy, and alongside the training stress itself contributes to fatigue. It is during the recovery period between training sessions, that your body repairs and rebuilds these muscles, making them stronger and more resilient. Not giving your body enough time to recover, and make the adaptations to the training stimulus can lead to over-training, increased risk of injury, increases in illness (i.e. colds, sinus infections, viruses) and compromised or completely derailed progress.

Recovery and adaptation to the training session _is the goal_.

To quote Dan John:

> _"Any idiot can make someone tired._
>
> _If you want a program to get you tired, do 10,000 jumping jacks. You will be tired, but you won't be better._
>
> _Training to get better at something is a whole different story."_

1. Sleep and Recovery

Rest and sleep are two key components of recovery. Your body needs time to rejuvenate, repair, and recharge. Adequate rest between workouts allows your muscles to recover and adapt to the stress placed upon them. Additionally, quality sleep is essential for hormone regulation, muscle repair, nervous system adaptations to training, and overall well-being. Aim for 7-9 hours of quality sleep per night and prioritize establishing a consistent sleep routine.

Cornerstones of a quality sleep routine include:

- Consistent bedtime and wake time + / - 30 minutes (this is absolutely vital, and the #1 thing we can do to help you)

- Avoiding stimulants like caffeine and alcohol in the 6 hours before bed. On average, it takes 3-6 hours to break down and process caffeine. Alcohol has a negative impact on deep sleep quality and dreaming

- Not eating an enormous meal before bed

- Keeping your room cool and dark

- Avoiding screens in the 2 hours before bed

- Having plants such as Lavender or Peace Lily in the bedroom (helps with air quality & relaxation)

2. Nutrition and Hydration

Proper nutrition and hydration play a vital role in the recovery process. Consuming a well-balanced diet rich in protein, carbohydrates, and essential nutrients provides the building blocks necessary for muscle repair and growth. Prioritize nutrient-dense foods such as lean meats, fish, whole grains, fruits, and vegetables. Adequate hydration is equally important, as dehydration can impair recovery and performance. Aim to drink at least

8-10 cups of water per day and adjust intake based on activity level and sweat rate.

On strength training days you may want to have an extra portion of protein before bed, as protein both slows digestion down, which can improve nutrient absorption and help supply building blocks your body needs to repair the muscles from that day's workout.

3. Active and Passive Recovery Methods

There are various active and passive recovery techniques that can expedite the recovery process and alleviate muscle soreness. Active recovery includes low-intensity activities such as light cardio or mobility exercises that promote blood flow and flush out metabolic waste. Examples include brisk walking, swimming, or cycling.

What many will find surprising, is that we can (and should) use strength training as an active recovery method! However, these Recovery Training Sessions follow a few rules, which we will discuss in Chapter 8.

Passive recovery methods, on the other hand, involve practices like foam rolling, massage therapy, or using cold or hot therapies to reduce inflammation and promote healing. Incorporating both active and passive recovery techniques into your routine can enhance overall recovery.

4. Stress and Relaxation

Stress, both physical and mental, can hinder the recovery process. Chronic stress can elevate cortisol levels, impede muscle repair, and compromise the immune system. Learning to manage and mitigate stress through relaxation techniques such as meditation, deep breathing exercises, or yoga can enhance recovery and overall well-being.

Experiment with different stress management techniques to find what works best for you. Consider dedicating time each day for relaxation activities.

These days, you can use an HRV measurement device to help you begin to better understand your stress ebbs and flows in life. The two I have found to be most accurate and precise are Morpheus (strap w/ App) and HRV4Training (app). However, it is extremely important to note that you will need to use an HRV measuring device for at least 2-3 weeks every single day to begin to have accurate scores.

But the power in the HRV measurement devices is in using them over a prolonged period of time i.e. daily, for a few months.

5. Breathwork

One of the most impactful and powerful things we can do to help you recover and perform better, is working on your breathing. Breathing has a significant effect on your Autonomic Nervous System. Working to add breathing as the first thing and last thing you do for each training session allows you to decrease stress, bring your heart rate lower, and allow you to better focus.

What many may not realize, is that practicing breathing better can improve joint positions and even restore range of motion!

From tight hamstrings and lower back tightness, to tight shoulders and stiff necks... we can use breathing exercises to help unlock these tight areas.

6. Listening to Your Body

Last, the art of recovery involves listening to your body and understanding its cues. Recognizing signs of over-training, fatigue, or injury is crucial to modify your training plan accordingly. Some signs to watch out for include decreased performance, persistent muscle soreness, increased resting heart rate, disrupted sleep, or changes in mood. If you notice any of these signs, it may be a signal to reduce intensity, increase rest days, or seek professional guidance. Prioritize self-care and give yourself permission to adjust your training plan as needed.

While we've seen many technologies burst onto the endurance sports and performance scene, still to date none of them have proven to be as accurate as an individual taking the time to get to know your own body, so you can better understand the signs and signals it is sending you.

Will there be days that you feel more mentally tired and drained than physically? Yes.

Can an accurate and precise HRV monitor help you more quickly understand that? Yes.

But as we say *"The buck stops with you."*

No technology should ever take over your own sensations and feelings. They can only be aids to our own feelings.

Take it from someone who has literally spent thousands of dollars on gadgets, doodads, and instruments in an attempt to try to shortcut learning these feelings - both for myself and those I coach.

Use these technologies and tools as an aid to help you lower your learning curve.

Think of them kind of like a *"cheat code"* like we used to have for those old arcades, or Nintendo games. Even if you know all the cheat codes, you still have to be at least a half-decent player to beat the game, or have a shot at it.

But so far, no one has found the ultimate cheat code for life, which means life is going to be serious.

So serious, indeed, that nobody gets out alive.

But we can improve the quality of life in your years, if we just learn how to listen to our bodies, and do things that stack the cards in our favor, whether we like them or not, consistently.

Why hello there daily fresh vegetables, bi-weekly strength training, and weekly recovery time/ relaxation time... How are *you* doin'?

Enhancing your Recovery

Let's take a look at a few easy ways that you can enhance your recovery, beyond the foundations we just discussed. Just keep in mind that the basics, while boring and seemingly simple, are what will get you 90% of what you need. The following should be added on top of these already consistent and regular foundations.

Mindset and Visualization

The mental aspect of recovery should not be overlooked. A positive mindset can significantly impact your recovery and overall performance. Engage in visualization exercises where you imagine yourself recovering effectively and performing at your best. This practice not only enhances motivation but also facilitates the mind-muscle connection, aiding in the recovery process. Embrace positive affirmations and create a mental space that supports healing and growth.

Practicing a gratitude mindset throughout the day has been shown by research studies to improve your mood, sleep, and even boost your immune system.

Optimizing Nutrient Timing

Timing your meals, and what makes up your meals strategically, can further enhance your recovery.

For quite some time, it was believed that consuming a combination of protein and carbohydrates within the first hour after your workout can kick start the muscle repair process. This window of opportunity, was referred to as the "anabolic window," and was thought to maximize the absorption of nutrients and promote faster recovery.

While certainly eating as close to your training finish as possible can offer benefits, such as peak insulin levels (which helps carbohydrate transport) and improved amino acid transport to the muscles, the most up-to-date research through 2023 has shown this window to be much longer (3 hours, even up to 5 hours) for men. Dr. Brad Schoenfeld has published a number of studies on the topic, if you'd like to read more.

However, for women, especially those in the second half of their menstrual cycle, this prime window seems to be at its peak for 30-45 minutes post-exercise.

For both women and men, it is recommended to eat between 25-40g of protein within the first 30-45 minutes after an exercise session. That said, there is research emerging which strongly suggests that you can also eat 20-30g of protein in the hour before your training session, which will have a similar effect. The only question is, *"Can you stomach that much protein close to a training session?"*

For those interested in diving deeper into the topic of women's needs, Dr. Stacy Sims has been putting much effort into sharing and making more widely known the differences in women and men throughout our training and adaptation processes since the 2010s and has produced several resources for female endurance athletes who are peri- and post-menopause to help you figure out a strategy of training and nutritional support.

Additionally, incorporating a small protein-rich snack before bed can provide a steady supply of amino acids to your muscles throughout the night. However, there are "better" kinds of protein for your evening snack, as they have a slower absorption rate, which plays to your favor while you sleep. Casein protein, or Cottage Cheese if you prefer something natural, can be a great pre-sleep protein snack. Eggs are another great protein source pre-bed.

Recovery Modalities

Beyond the traditional recovery techniques, several recovery modalities can be considered. These modalities include compression therapy, such as wearing compression garments or using compression boots, which may enhance blood flow and reduce muscle soreness. Another modality is contrast therapy, where you alternate between hot and cold treatments to improve circulation and reduce inflammation. A regular massage by a skilled massage therapist, when done regularly, can pay off in spades! One-off massages here and there can certainly help you when you have had a large training load. However regular monthly or every-other month massages by the same masseuse will allow them to develop a feel and better understanding of how your body holds stress and deals with different kinds of training loads, thus helping you become wiser in how to best prepare for and address those issues.

Experiment with these modalities to find what works best for your body.

It is important to note that the more you use a recovery modality (cold water, compression boots, etc.) the less of an effect it may have over time.

By no means am I saying any of these will become useless. But I say that you should aim to be specific and strategic with using tools and technologies to aid recovery. These each certainly can have a place in your recovery approaches.

One approach, which we will discuss in Chapter 8, is a Recovery Strength Training session.

Yup!

You read that right.

When done appropriately, strength training can be a way to recover from your riding! However, as you'll learn, there are a few rules that need to be followed to make sure it's a recovery session.

While I had used recovery strength training sessions with my aspiring professional riders and athletes, I had been hesitant to have my masters riders use them mid-season. There was no good reason, aside from the fear (yes, real, genuine fear) from the riders that mid-season strength training, especially leading towards a peak event or few weeks of riding would leave them sore and too tired to ride...

That was one big miscalculation on my end, as these riders, riders like you, whom have found the biggest benefit from these strength sessions, and who have been filling my inbox every summer with messages asking *"How can I get results like Carl?"* and *"Help me ride (and look) like Terry- she is just a whole different rider since starting with you!"*

We'll get to those sessions and how to do them in Chapter 8, but it's incredibly important for you to understand that this book has been put together in a way to help you not only to lift heavy, but to see better riding and quality of life from your time hitting the weights.

As we've discussed in this chapter, you cannot improve your riding, strength, or really anything to do with the human body, without giving it (your body) the down time, sleep, and nutrients (physical and mental) to recover and adapt to the training stresses you've placed on it.

By mastering the art of recovery, you will not only enhance your physical performance but also reduce the risk of injury, promote longevity in your strength training journey, and achieve sustainable progress. Incorporate these recovery techniques, practices, and modalities into your routine, and enjoy the all-encompassing benefits it brings. Remember, recovery is not a luxury, but a necessity for optimal performance and well-being... But it all begins and is heavily reliant on the fundamentals of:

- Quality sleep with regular bedtimes and waking times

- Proper nutrition with dark, leafy greens, lean proteins, and healthy fats as your pillars

- Seeking training consistency, not tenacity

- Focusing your strength trainings on technique and how you perform a movement, using RPE or RIR as your guides

- Making down-time from training / proper recovery a non-negotiable

- Choosing to practice gratitude daily

- Enjoying the process, not just the end goal.

Chapter Six

Balancing Act
Strength and Flexibility

In this chapter, we delve deeper into the critical importance of finding the perfect balance between strength and flexibility in your fitness routine. By integrating flexibility exercises to complement strength training, you can achieve a holistic and injury-resistant approach to fitness.

One of the more common thoughts that seems to have stuck around, is that everyone needs flexibility training. Some kind of stretching practice or routine. While the idea is a good one, Our understanding of the human body and how it works has progressed significantly.

Most notably, two items stick out as being significant in the discussion around flexibility training:

1. The research has trended to show that static stretches (held longer than 20 seconds) decreases power and strength, as well as can increase the risk of injury if done before a sporting event or performance

2. How we are only now progressing in the understanding of the fascial systems in the body and quite how much they contribute and aid in movement, and that it is not just about *"tight muscles"*

Integrating flexibility exercises to complement strength training for a holistic and injury-resistant approach

Integrating flexibility exercises into your routine not only helps improve joint mobility, increase range of motion, and enhance overall flexibility, but also plays a vital role in injury prevention. Engaging in strength training alone can lead to tightened muscles, restricted mobility, and imbalances in muscle development. These imbalances can potentially cause poor posture, compromised movement patterns, and a higher risk of injuries. By incorporating flexibility exercises, you can counteract these issues, ensuring that all muscle groups are equally strengthened and stretched, helping them to come to ideal resting lengths and to be able to 'tune' the system to work better.

Understanding Muscular Stiffness & Tightness

One important thing that you absolutely need to know about flexibility and muscle stiffness, is that there is a good amount of "stiffness" at the joints of the body which are driven by the bodies subconscious protective mechanisms, built to help you avoid injuring yourself.

This is very clear when one looks at someone who has gone to see an orthopedic surgeon for a joint issue. When on the exam table in the office, they show stiffness and inability to get into certain ranges of motion. But once they are under anesthesia, there are no limitations.

Why is that?

This strange occurrence is due to the brain's interaction with the muscles, bones, joints, and fascia of the body "telling it" that there is a problem at that joint. So the brain (without your knowledge) shuts down muscles in that region, in order to keep you from causing catastrophic damage to that joint, or due to repeatedly using the muscles through a smaller range of motion (why hello there cycling).

It all dials down to the 3 jobs the muscles have within the body, in relation to movement.

Job #1: Protect a joint from injury

Muscles will *"shut down"* in order to protect a joint from injury. While sometimes we may be aware of an imbalance at a joint or an issue, this is mostly done at a subconscious level, thus what happens when we're under anesthesia and the surgeon is able to access that range of motion that we didn't while awake.

Job #2: To stabilize a joint while an adjacent joint moves

(i.e. your biceps keeping your elbow stable while you raise your arm overhead)

Job #3: To move a joint

As we all know and understand.

Understanding these three jobs must be done in this order, will help you get better results from your flexibility and mobility work, as you'll be able to start thinking a little more about the big picture, instead of just focusing on *"the tight muscle."*

Begin With The End In Mind

When it comes to flexibility exercises, there are various options to consider. Stretching exercises, such as static stretching or dynamic stretching, have been commonly used to improve flexibility.

In order to figure out what kind of stretching is most appropriate or best for you, we'll need to begin with the end in mind:

- What is your goal for this specific session?

- What properties are you trying to improve or change?

- What is your long-term goal?

We need to understand first where you are trying to go, and from there we can begin to look at the different kinds of stretching, and which of them would best serve you, and how to apply them.

Different Types of Stretching

Static stretching involves holding a stretch position for a prolonged period, typically between 15 and 60 seconds. This type of stretching is thought to help lengthen the muscles and connective tissues, improving flexibility and reducing muscle tension. It is commonly performed as part of the cool-down phase after a workout or as a standalone routine on rest days.

Once we get into our 50s, it can be beneficial to add a short stand-alone static stretching session once or twice a week. Why in our 50s? Well, for one, our 50s is when both men and women tend to really see and feel the effects of their lifestyle choices over the years. Having a static stretching session once a week may help you maintain good ranges of motion, tune into 'hot spots' where you commonly hold tension, as well as serve as a nice recovery session.

But static stretching alone will not do the job.

You absolutely must include strength training to help keep those muscles working well through that newfound range of motion and to address the root cause of the muscles being tight... which tend to be posture or use/ neglect related.

Dynamic stretching, on the other hand, involves active movements that either mimic the motions of a specific activity or sport, or which help prepare the body and its tissues to perform well in upcoming tasks or exercises. This form of stretching helps improve flexibility, muscle coordination, proprioception, balance, and overall athletic performance. Dynamic stretches are often incorporated into the warm-up phase before engaging in more intense exercises. They involve controlled movements that bring your body through a full range of motion while gradually increasing the intensity and speed.

When building a strength training program for performance, we also will use dynamic stretches in between exercises, as well as breathing exercises, to help improve your ability to perform the main lift, which it is paired with. There is an art and a science to this programming, as the coach or practitioner needs to have a sound understanding of how the body for that rider is moving, what their underlying movement strategies are, and where they are trying to take that person to as far as movement.

Both types of stretching can be beneficial in improving flexibility and mobility, but the choice depends on your specific needs and preferences, as well as where and when they are each being applied. Some individuals may find that static stretching is more effective for their body, while others may prefer the dynamic approach. Experimenting with both can help you determine which form of stretching resonates best with your body and yields the desired results. A good general rule to follow is to try something for two weeks and see if it has a noticeable effect on your desired outcome.

This is where static stretching can be a bit tricky, as many people will feel more range of motion or simply "better" immediately after a static stretching session... But if we see that you've not improved your ability to keep better position outside of the static stretching session we will want to look to add some kind of strength or dynamic stretching activity to your routine, which helps move you along to where you do feel better outside of your stretching sessions.

Another option to explore is yoga. Yoga not only focuses on flexibility but also incorporates strength-building elements. Yoga poses, or asanas, work on different muscle groups, helping to increase flexibility, balance, and stability. The flowing sequences and deep stretches in yoga promote both active and passive flexibility, allowing you to develop the strength necessary to support your newfound flexibility. Additionally, yoga encourages body awareness, mindfulness, and deep breathing techniques, which can further enhance the mind-body connection and overall well-being.

It is very important to note that when adding yoga our goal is not to become flexy-bendy like those who only practice yoga. But instead, the goal is to help you learn where your body is in space, how to keep tension where you need it, when you need it, and to use breathing to relax or fire up specific muscles.

There have been plenty of cyclists who have hit yoga hard with the mindset of becoming as flexible as possible, only to see their on-bike performances plummet. As we discussed in Chapter 4 Lift Smart, Lift Heavy, we absolutely must keep in mind the specific properties which are necessary for you to succeed in your sport. And for cycling, yes, we do often see the need to improve the rider's ability to extend the hip, upper back, and shoulders, but more is not better!

You want just enough flexibility, with the ability to produce and control stiffness where you need it, when you need it, so you can pedal with power down the road, trail, or track.

Pilates is another fantastic option to integrate flexibility and strength training. Developed by Joseph Pilates, this exercise method focuses on improving core strength, flexibility, and overall body control. Pilates exercises target the deep stabilizing muscles of the abdomen, back, and pelvic floor, which helps in finding balance between strength and flexibility.

It's important to note that integrating flexibility exercises should be tailored to your specific needs and goals. Consulting with a qualified professional or trainer can help you identify areas of your body that could benefit from increased flexibility and create a plan that suits your unique requirements. They can also guide you in performing exercises correctly, ensuring that you maximize the benefits and minimize the risk of injury.

Remember, finding the right balance between strength and flexibility is not about becoming excessively flexible or impossibly strong, but rather about achieving functional fitness that supports your overall well-being. Gradually increasing the intensity and duration of your flexibility exercises allows your muscles and connective tissues to adapt and become more resilient over time.

By prioritizing the integration of flexibility exercises into your strength training routine, you are equipping your body with the tools it needs to maintain optimal performance, prevent injuries, enhance recovery, and promote overall longevity in your fitness journey. Embrace this balancing act and unlock the incredible benefits that come from nurturing both strength and flexibility.

Chapter Seven

Nutrition For Masters

Fueling Your Body

In this chapter, we will discuss the essential aspects of nutrition for masters athletes. As we age, it becomes even more important to address our dietary considerations to support muscle growth, aid in recovery, and promote overall well-being.

By no means is this a complete overview, but rather I'll just touch on the very foundations, and give you some very general suggestions on where to start. I am a strength & cycling coach by trade, not a dietician. It is always best to consult with an RD/LD to help make sure you're on point with your nutrition and dietary needs.

Addressing dietary considerations to support muscle growth, recovery, and overall well-being:

Masters athletes have unique dietary considerations due to changes in metabolism, hormone levels, and overall body composition.

Adequate nutrition plays a pivotal role in supporting muscle growth, optimizing recovery, and maintaining overall health.

By following the right dietary strategies, we can enhance our performance, minimize the risk of injury, and achieve our fitness goals.

Understanding your body's needs

As masters athletes, our bodies have different requirements compared to younger individuals. Slower metabolic rates and decreased muscle mass may necessitate adjusting our calorie intake.

For females who are peri- or post-menopausal, strength training has been at the forefront of helping to fight back against the loss of lean muscle mass.

Men also have a lot to gain by adding regular, consistent, year-round strength training 2-3 days a week for overall health and abilities, but in order to support this new training focus we need to ensure we are getting enough nutrients to maintain and build muscle mass, support our immune system, and keep our energy levels high.

Being mindful of our body's needs allows us to optimize our physical performance and feel our best.

Balancing macronutrients

The first step in fueling your body effectively is to balance your macronutrients - carbohydrates, proteins, and fats. Each of these macronutrients plays a crucial role in our overall health. For masters athletes, it is essential to strike a balance that provides the right amount of energy without overloading on any specific macronutrient.

Carbohydrates

Carbohydrates are the primary fuel source for athletes, providing energy for training and competition. Focus on consuming complex carbohydrates such as whole grains, fruits, and vegetables, which provide sustained energy and essential nutrients, as well as a range of all important fiber, something which most Americans fall very short on in their daily nutrition choices.

Proteins

Protein is essential for muscle repair and growth. As masters athletes, aiming for an intake of around 1.4-1.8 grams of protein per kilogram of body weight per day is recommended. Include lean sources of protein like poultry, fish, beans, and legumes in your meals. Additionally, incorporating plant-based protein sources like tofu, tempeh, lentils, and quinoa can provide a variety of amino acids necessary for muscle repair.

That said, if you are consuming mostly vegan sources of protein, you will want to seek good sources of the amino acid Leucine. Studies suggest that it plays an integral role in muscle tissue repair, but tends to be best found in non-vegan foods. Just something for you to chew on when looking at your protein sources.

Fats

Healthy fats are crucial for hormone production, joint health, and overall well-being. Opt for foods rich in monounsaturated and polyunsaturated fats such as avocados, nuts, seeds, and olive oil. Omega-3 fatty acids, found in fatty fish like salmon and trout, are particularly beneficial for heart health and reducing inflammation in the body.

Addressing muscle growth and recovery

Supporting muscle growth and aiding recovery is of utmost importance for masters athletes. We'll discuss the importance of protein intake and how proper distribution throughout the day can enhance muscle protein synthesis. Additionally, we'll explore the benefits of including essential amino acids and Branched-Chain Amino Acids (BCAAs) in your diet to aid in recovery and optimize muscle repair.

Essential Amino Acids

These are key components of protein that our bodies cannot produce on their own. Consuming foods rich in essential amino acids like eggs, dairy, quinoa, lean meats, and legumes can support muscle growth and recovery. For plant-based athletes, combining different plant-based protein sources (complementary proteins) can ensure a more even amino acid profile.

While it had been thought for many years that vegan sources of protein are *"incomplete proteins,"* it turns out that is a myth which had been proven false over 40 years ago (in 1981, by the very author who had proposed the idea), but has been proliferated for many years by the mass media.

Rather than being *"incomplete,"* vegan sources have a different amino acid profile than meat and dairy sources, with some amino acids not being found as plentiful or easily as in meat and dairy sources. For example, Luciene, mentioned above, is one which is not found as plentiful in plant-based sources. Due to its specific role in different processes in the body, if you are plant-based, you'll want to put a little more effort into making sure you're hitting your needs.

Branched-Chain Amino Acids (BCAAs)

BCAAs, which include leucine, isoleucine, and valine, play a vital role in muscle protein synthesis. They have been shown to enhance recovery, reduce muscle soreness, and prevent muscle breakdown. You can find BCAAs in foods like chicken, fish, eggs, and whey protein supplements. However, it is important to note that obtaining BCAAs through whole food sources is generally more beneficial than relying solely on supplements.

Come to think of it, except when necessitated by a medical professional due to a proper deficiency one may have, eating whole foods is better than taking a supplement. Whole foods offer us a host of benefits beyond specific amino acids and offer far more to nourish our bodies (and souls, and social life) than popping a pill, taking a few drops, or mixing up a powdered drink.

Choosing nutrient-dense foods

As masters athletes, our focus should be on consuming nutrient-dense foods that provide a wide range of vitamins, minerals, and antioxidants. These foods support overall health, enhance recovery, and optimize performance.

Fruits and vegetables

Aim for a variety of colorful fruits and vegetables to obtain essential vitamins, minerals, and antioxidants. These foods also provide dietary fiber, which aids digestion and helps maintain a healthy weight, and contribute to a healthy, robust gut microbiome, something which we are just now beginning to explore and research. Consider including dark leafy greens like kale and spinach, as they are rich in nutrients like iron and folate.

Cruciferous vegetables like brussell sprouts, red radishes, arugula, kohlrabi, cabbage and the like offer a whole host of wonderful benefits for your body, and should be a regular part of your diet.

Whole grains

Opt for whole grains such as brown rice, quinoa, whole wheat bread, and oatmeal. These complex carbohydrates provide sustained energy release and are rich in fiber and important nutrients. Whole grains also contain phytochemicals that offer various health benefits, including reducing the risk of chronic diseases.

Buckwheat, spelt, and amaranth, while not as popular as oatmeal and whole wheat, offer different textures and nutrient profiles, as well as add a pinch of adventure and excitement to your weekly diet. While you may not necessarily like the taste of each of these, it's important to try new foods and expand your palate, as variety is (after all) the spice of life. And you never know, it is quite possible that a grain that you had never heard of before turns out to be your new favorite!

Lean proteins

Choose lean sources of protein such as chicken, turkey, fish, tofu, beans, and legumes. These options are low in saturated fat and rich in essential amino acids. If you follow a plant-based diet, ensure you are combining different plant-based protein sources to obtain a variety of amino acids to fill out your amino acid profile, as noted above. Again, it's best to consult with an RD/LD on nutrition and diet.

Healthy fats

Include foods like avocados, nuts, seeds, olive oil, and fatty fish (salmon, mackerel, trout) to obtain healthy fats, omega-3 fatty acids, and vitamin E. Omega-3 fatty acids have anti-inflammatory properties and promote cardiovascular health. Avoid trans fats and minimize consumption of saturated fats found in processed foods and animal products.

Hydration and electrolyte balance

Proper hydration is crucial for masters athletes, as it helps maintain optimal performance, regulate body temperature, and support the health of our joints and muscles. What you may not know, is that technically speaking, blood is a connective tissue. That's right! Blood is the superhighway of the body, helping to deliver messages via hormones, nutrients and oxygen where needed, immune cells to where they are needed to fight an infection, as well to remove wastes and byproducts out of the body or to the proper organ to be removed from the body.

Staying hydrated throughout the day is vital, and while most of us will give it special attention during intense training sessions and competition, we really need to make it a regular habit. Changes in blood volume or makeup can have huge effects on our abilities to train and perform. Even a 1% drop in blood volume has far-reaching negative implications for your performance, as the heart and cardiovascular system need to work harder, in order to deliver the oxygen and nutrients where needed and to clear out the byproducts and waste.

Research done since the start of the 2000s has shown that women, in particular, face challenges with the blood plasma levels during the second half of their menstrual cycle -days 15-28 if you follow the 'standard 28 day cycle'- (I've yet to work with a female who has a 28 day cycle. Your menstrual cycle can be anywhere from 21-40 days). Dr Stacy Sims has done a lot to promote the unique needs of women who are training for sports, and I'd recommend that you pick up *Roar*, her first book, which covers pretty much everything you'd want to learn more.

For those who are perimenopause (the time when your cycle becomes more irregular as the hormones change in the body leading up to menopause, which can last as long as 10 years) or post-menopause, Dr. Sims book *Next Level* offers some really great insights to the changes your body is undergoing, and strategies which you can use to help you feel, look, and move better.

A general guideline for daily fluid intake is to consume at least 2-3 liters of water, depending on your body size and weight, and more during periods of increased activity or in hot and cold weather. The cold weather is where many tend to fall short, as our awareness of drinking tends to decrease. However, our need for water to help us maintain an even body temperature increases, as we tend to spend our time near dry heat sources like air conditioning or radiators, which pulls even more water from the body.

A best practice is to track your water intake by using a bottle to track how much you've drank throughout the day. There are even bottles that are equipped with bluetooth and connect with an app, so you can get a notification on your phone or smartwatch that you're behind on your drinking! I don't know about you, but this is way too much for me. I wasn't all that interested in George Jetson's video watch, as much as I was the flying cars... you can have your bluetooth connected bottles reminding you to drink, I'll wait for those flying cars (and talking dogs).

Additionally, maintaining electrolyte balance by consuming foods rich in electrolytes, such as bananas, coconut water, and leafy green vegetables, can benefit overall performance and recovery. While there are a whole host of electrolyte drinks out there these days, it is my opinion that far too many endurance athletes have lost the very foundations of a healthy, real-food based diet, and are too dependent on supplements.

Not that supplements are not useful or are to be avoided. Supplements certainly have a role to play. . .

To **supplement** a regular, healthy diet.

Check your foundations before you go spending a few hundred bucks for the latest and greatest designer electrolyte mix. A regular supply of season fruits and vegetables often will hit the spot for the vast majority of your training year needs, with electrolyte supplements being useful for those really long or intense sessions, or when the weather has your freeing your important bits off, or sweating like Slimer from Ghostbusters (thank you Bill Murray, I will take that special this week for proton charging and storage of the beast.)

The Changed Energy Paradigm

What we once believed, is not really true. . . For years, decades, centuries perhaps, it has been thought that *"as long as I eat more, I can train more,"* and as endurance athletes we bought in, hook, line, and stinker, err, sinker.

But the most current studies, which have looked at some of the remaining hunter-gatherers in the world as compared to those of us in our fabricated *"urban zoos"* burn exactly the same amount of energy as a baseline (when controlled for body size).

That's right!

Those Hadza hunters and gatherers in the plains of Africa burn pretty much the exact same calories that a couch potato in Chicago watching Seinfeld reruns does, at rest.

Now you may be thinking *"at rest,"* so that means if I'm more active I'll burn more. But that's the biggest misunderstanding of them all! Our bodies, over the time of human existence, has become the most high-performing metabolic engine known to man, as our hypothalamus works to keep our daily energy expenditure as close to that baseline as possible on a day-to-day basis.

It does this by adjusting up or down the various functions that happen without our thought or attention: Immune system function, reproductive status (i.e. women who do not eat enough lose their period), spleen function, just to name a few.

In his groundbreaking book *Burn: New Research Blows The Lid Off How We Really Burn Calories, Lose Weight, And Stay Healthy*, Dr. Herman Pontzer shares unequivocal evidence that what we thought we knew about metabolism, is grossly miscalculated.

Why do I say miscalculated and not *"wrong?"*

Because there is still so much more that we need to study and learn about this. But the evidence he has presented and shared is undeniable, and trends right in line with what dieticians and coaches have known for years: If you want to lose weight, more exercise is not the answer. You have to eat less than you burn each day, period.

This is a critical point that we as masters athletes have to understand, in large part because many still believe that riding more will help them lose weight, and specifically body fat.

It just doesn't work like that.

You must eat less, in order to change your body composition - but you need to eat enough of the important things in order to keep your body able to show up to your ride or strength training session recovered, adapted to your last training, and able to maintain essential body functions.

But there is a point where more physical activity actually eats into the energy available for our body's ability to run all the necessary operations to stay healthy.

And this is where it is important to understand the constrained energy model, and how our activities change what happens with the energy you eat and how you burn each calorie.

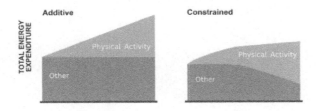

This is a much deeper topic than I can cover here, and I recommend picking up Dr. Pontzer's book to learn more about the Constrained Energy Model, the updated view on how our metabolism works, and how you can better adjust your own nutrition strategies to see the results you are after.

Stay consistent with your nutrition, focusing on nailing the fundamentals of fresh produce (vegetables and fruits), with an emphasis on fresh, in-season, and if possible local , as well as 1.2-1.8g/kg of protein a day, and appropriate amounts of healthy fats, and hydrate properly to support your athletic performance and overall well-being as a masters athlete.

It may be simple, but it is not easy... Especially as an endurance athlete being sold all of these sports nutrition supplements. Master the fundamentals in your daily diet, being consistent with them, and you will likely be very surprised as to how little and how infrequently you actually need those supplements.

Chapter Eight

Tailoring Your Training Plan

Crafting a personalized strength training program that aligns with cycling goals and individual capabilities is essential for optimizing performance and avoiding injuries. In this chapter, we will talk about the different aspects of designing a training plan that suits your needs and elevates your cycling abilities.

Understanding Personalization: Aligning Strength Training with Cycling Goals and Capabilities

Crafting a personalized strength training program for cycling requires considering both your cycling goals and individual capabilities. By aligning your strength training with your specific goals, whether it's improving sprinting power, endurance, climbing ability, or overall performance, you can direct your efforts towards the areas that require improvement.

Additionally, understanding your individual capabilities, including your current strength levels, ability to create appropriate stiffness to create more effective and efficient power, mobility, and any existing limitations, is crucial.

This knowledge enables you to design a program that is tailored to your unique needs, allowing for progress while minimizing the risk of injuries and maximizing the returns from your strength training.

Remember that everyone's starting point and capacity for development are different, so it's essential to embrace your own journey and work within your abilities. You may be a highly advanced cyclist, with well over 10 years of riding under your belt, but a true beginner in strength training.

In order for you to get on the quickest, most efficient, and sustainable path to improved performances and quality of life, you must check your ego at the door.

Yes, we are going to lift heavy sh*t, but we are going to be wise in both how we program and execute that lifting.

Building A Training Plan

Just as having a plan and program for your riding helps you to see better results, it is especially true with strength training.

While some cyclists are looking to strength train to boost their performances, thus the title of my first book *Strength Training for Cycling Performance*, all cyclists would do extremely well to follow some kind of structured approach to their strength training.

Reason being, is that while we may not necessarily want (or need) all of our energy systems to be at their absolute best in order to enjoy our riding and life off the bike, strength training offers us huge benefits far above and beyond just riding. But in order to reap those benefits beyond the "*newbie gains"* which we will talk about in a moment, you absolutely must have a progressive strength training program.

Sure, you could hit the weights and just wing it, but by putting even just a little structure into your strength training can give you massive rewards, as well as make it a less monotonous task.

Here's how you can look at your strength training programming to help you *"guide the ship."*

Macrocycle - Big Picture. Where do you want to go over the next 1-2 years?

Mesocycle - What do the next 2-6 weeks (and sometimes with cyclists 8 weeks) look like on the path to get there?

Microcycle - What does this week look like?

Training day - What does this one training day look like?

It can be tempting to just hit the gym and repeat a workout "until" you either see improvement or get bored of the workout, however if you're looking for strength training to help keep you active, able-bodied, and able to ride strong for many decades to come, you'll be spinning your wheels, making yourself tired, more than making progress.

This, in fact, is one of the biggest complaints I've heard over the last 5 years from the cyclists who come to me seeking a better way: *"I've been strength training for the last 2 years, lifting heavy sh*t, but I'm still pretty much where I was after my first 6 months. I saw some great increases in those first 6 months or so, but since then, nothing!"*

These first 6 months gains (really 4-8 months), are what are often referred to as *"newbie gains."* That's because in those first few months of weight training you can pretty much walk into the gym and sneeze, and you'll see some improvements (I'm mostly kidding. But please cover your mouth when you sneeze... not with your hands, that's just gross, you touch everything in the weight room with those hands!). These improvements come from the body adapting to a new training stimulus. So long as you show up and do some work, you'll see some pretty nice improvements.

In large part, it is those very "*newbie gains*" that keep many cyclists and triathletes who hit the gym each winter, thinking that they're making progress. When in fact if you look year to year, those gains tend to be less and less, and if you took a break from strength training over your riding season, you've never really gotten to the same levels of strength as you had in previous years.

Often dismissed with the thought of *"Yup, I must be gettin' older,"* it's actually due in large part to the body having already adapted to that stimulus.

The body says *"Oh, this again? Been there, done that, got the t-shirt."*

We already mentioned this back in Chapter 4, Anatoliy Bondarchuk's insight that once you use a training approach, whether at the right time or not, you've lost out twice on the adaptations that can occur.

But there is hope, and a better way!

Periodizing your strength program throughout the training year.

To Periodize, or Not To Periodize... That Is Not Even A Question!

Way back in Chapter 1, I mentioned how some folks argue that you cannot periodize strength training for cyclists, or that *"periodization doesn't work for cyclists."* In fact, I've seen this from several very good cycling coaches who mean well.

However, they've not yet developed a deep understanding of what strength training can do, nor how to best implement it throughout a training year, and are missing the very bedrock of strength training: to improve your bodies ability to be strong & resilient, so that you can continue to perform in your given sport.

That said, I get it!

I too went through that growth stage as a coach thinking that the periodization of strength couldn't work for cyclists. We have numerous events throughout the season which are important (either to us personally, or as points for qualification for leveling up), as well as a lot of time spent traveling, which often means not having access to anything beyond the rider's body, and a few bands or TRX which they brought along with them.

How can we stay consistent when our time is spent riding our bikes (we are endurance athletes after all), traveling, and racing?

But, in fact, these obstacles only change HOW we perform the strength training.

Now let's be honest here, if you're meant to be doing Max Strength work and all you've got with you are a few bands....

Well, we aren't in a position where we'll get the ideal training stimulus. However, there is always _something_ that we can train well, regardless of where you are, and our job in these instances is to ensure that you're making progress towards the bigger picture.

So the question is not *"Is periodization something we should do?"* Rather, it is not a question at all, but instead the realization that *"**Classical Periodization** does not fit our sports needs."*

There are over 40 different kinds of periodizations that one can use that have been developed over the years, and in fact one of them is called *"Competition to Competition Periodization,"* which addresses this very challenge.

To package this up and tie it off with a pretty bow and get to the good stuff, we'll put it this way:

Periodization is like having a GPS device.

The Macrocycle is choosing your destination, the Mesocycle is deciding if you want to take the scenic route or most direct route for this part of the ride, the Microcycle is your next turn, and your Daily training is the fuel gauge, check engine light, gas & brake pedals, and speedometer.

We use each of these to get you to your desired destination.

Otherwise, we're literally Alice in Wonderland...

> *"Would you tell me, please, which way I ought to go from here?"*
>
> *"That depends a good deal on where you want to get to,"* said the Cat.
>
> *"I don't much care where-"* said Alice.

"Then it doesn't matter which way you go," said the Cat.

Your end goal does not need to be measured as performance in an event, a certain speed, or a power output. It could be something as simple as *"I want to be able to do my own landscaping when I'm 80 still"* or *"I want to feel better at 74 than I did at 54."*

High performance is all relative to what **_you_** determine it is.

But in order to get there, you'll need to focus on one thing at a time.

A word of advice: After having been coaching for over 25 years, I can tell you without a doubt that the worst thing you can say when asked about a strength training or fitness goal is the very general *"I want to be stronger and healthier."*

To have this broad of a goal means we will accomplish very little, as all we want to do, essentially, is to play in the ocean... an ocean... any ocean.

I don't know about you, but I'd rather play in the ocean somewhere warm, with a nice quiet beach, some great riding close by, and amazing food.

Not the Arctic Ocean.

If you're having a really tough time deciding, simply make up a goal for 3 months in the future and work towards that.

To paraphrase Jim Rohn:

> *"When do you begin to build the house?*
>
> *When it's finished!*

You have a clear, sharp idea of what it will look like. So sharp, in fact, that when you take your best friend for a tour on the lot of land, you bump your elbow on the kitchen counter."

Looking At The Training Year

Let's look at what a general training year might look like here.

But I'm going to be incredibly honest and blunt: I do not have THE answer for you and your specific needs.

What we are about to go over here is a very broad generalization of what a training year may look like. All this should do for you, is provide a framework, or a blank canvas, on which you should be working.

There are *"guardrails"* so to speak, helping you understand a few very important points:

Heavy lifting is best done (for masters athletes) in the late base period all the way into mid-season.

This pretty much goes directly against what many are doing these days, but I have found over the last 15+ years of working with masters cyclists and triathletes, that the overwhelming majority do extremely well with this, and see their best performances year in and year out following this recipe.

To be clear, when I say "heavy lifting" I'm referring to sets of 3-6 repetitions per set. The weights, as you surely know by this point of the book, are based on RPE, not what you have done *"to date."*

You're probably thinking I'm crazy, but as you'll learn shortly here, we actually use these heavy weight training sessions to super-boost your recovery and adaptations from your rides.

It's pretty magical stuff, and once you've tried it, you'll probably never go back to the old way.

1. **Power, explosiveness, and proximal stiffness training needs to be year-round**

   While it can be beneficial to go through a more dedicated "power" or "explosive" strength training block leading up to a key event or prime riding season, for endurance athletes over the age of 50, failure to train these traits regularly throughout the training year means that you lose a large portion of these capabilities year-to year. Joe Friel discusses exactly this in his book *Faster After 50*, if you'd like to dig deeper into this.

2. **Less Is More**

   When it comes to strength training, we absolutely, positively, do not want or need to smash you in the trainings.
   Unlike VO2 Max or FTP building efforts on the bike, where you absolutely must find that limit and push it in order to see improvements, strength training is a long-game. Each strength session should roughly fall into the overall RPE range of 5-7 (on a 1-10 scale), where you did high-quality work, but you can bounce back within 24-36 hours.

Overview Of A Training Year

Back in Chapter 1 we had a general overview of what a training year would look like for you, using a northern hemisphere athlete as an example. If you're in the southern hemisphere, you'll need to appropriately adjust the months to match the season i.e. October = April (your beginning of autumn), etc.

Let's get a little more detailed with pairing the cycling periods with the strength periods, starting with the end of the season (fall):

October:

2 weeks

Transition (on-bike) + Anatomical Adaptations (Strength)

November-January:

12 weeks
Base (On-bike, either 3*4 week blocks, or 2*6 week blocks) + Hypertrophy (Strength, 2*6 week blocks)

February-April:

12 weeks
Late Base into Early Build (On-bike, either 4*3 week blocks, 3*4 week blocks, or 2*6 week blocks) + Max Strength (Strength, either 4*3 week blocks, 3*4 week blocks)

May-June:

8 Weeks
Build (On-bike, either 2*4 week or 2*3 + 1*2 blocks) + Sport Specification (Strength, either 2*4 week or 2*3 + 1*2 blocks)

July:

4 Weeks
Peak (On-bike, 4 weeks) + Maintenance (Strength, 4 weeks)

August- September:

8 weeks
Maintenance (On-bike, either 2*4 week or 2*3 + 1*2 blocks) + Max Strength/ Hypertrophy (Strength, either 2*4 week or 2*3 + 1*2 blocks)

You will probably notice that there is a good bit of crossover between the programming in-season for riding + strength training.

While this does tend to happen more frequently than not, there are plenty of times where strength training will be cut a week short, or be extended a week (or two) longer, due to that specific rider's needs, abilities to recover & adapt, and life circumstances.

It all depends on what is going on in that rider's life, how well they are doing on the bike, as well as their overall energy and health status on a day to day and week to week basis.

If you're finishing week 2 of what is supposed to be a 4 week strength training block, but you're feeling a bit more worn down and your riding is a bit lackluster, you are probably better off moving your deload week forward to be week 3, instead of week 4. As you'll learn here in a minute, that means beginning your next block earlier.

Let's take a look at the Mesocycles, what they would look like. As you'll learn shortly, the last week of the Mesocycles will "deload" you by decreasing the total volume (number of reps x number of sets performed). However, this deload week will often, but not always, having you feeling strong, and able to move heavier weights at the same RPE as the week previous.

This is one way in which you are now lifting heavy sh*t in a far more intelligent and promoting fashion!

1. You've practiced and learned how to perform each exercise with better postures and techniques.

2. Layering strength on top of these movement improvements by adding repetitions at lower loads (due to how many quality sets and repetitions you are required to do), allowing the nervous system as well as the fascia, tendons, and other tissues involved the time and energy needed to strengthen and improve.

3. In the last week of the block you can lift some pretty heavy stuff at a similar RPE to weeks before, with far better technique, all while building you up, not blowing you to smithereens!

Let's take a look at how to do it intelligently.

Breaking down the Mesocycles

Mesocycles, those 2-6 (and even 8) week long blocks, are the deep foundations of a strength training program. It is with these blocks where you make the biggest adaptive changes to your body and its abilities.

These blocks are where you really focus on telling your body the exact adaptations and changes that you want it to make.

Want to get stronger at lifting heavy things, focus on just that for 2-6 weeks.

But, this does NOT mean that you're off to do heavy sets of 3s or 5s each week in the gym. There is a rhyme and a reason to how you'll want to structure each week within the mesocycle.

To make this easy to understand, we are going to use a 4 week training block as an example. This is how pretty much every single cycling and triathlon coach is taught how to build programs, and there is a reason for it: 4 weeks is simply a single month, and thus easy to build out and learn how to balance things.

Week 1 is a beginning week, due to the fact that these are new exercises, so chances are high that you'll be sore since these are a new stimulus to the body.

- For week 1, we'll do 2 sets of 10 repetitions.

- For week 2, we'll do 3 sets of 10 repetitions.

- Week 3 will be 3 sets of 12 repetitions.

- Week 4 will be 2 sets of 8 repetitions.

With this approach, we are building up the volume of work that you're doing each week, allowing you to increase the demand on the body in a way that you can get the muscle and tissue adaptations you need, without destroying yourself or your athlete.

Now you may be wondering what the weights would look like for each of these weeks. For weeks 1-3, the weights would be something around an RPE of 6-7 (medium), where you are able to complete each set with great technique and at the end of each set, still have a few high-quality repetitions in the tank.

The fun part of this is that due to the increase in total repetitions done, the weight most likely will not change much week to week. But rather, will stay the same as you work to move more total weight with great technique.

Training smarter, not harder!

But on week 4, which is technically a "deload" week, because you have far less volume, and even less sets, your RPE of 6-7 will most likely be a heavier weight.

So you're lifting heavier sh*t on your deload week, feeling like a rock star, and looking extremely solid in your technique.

Talk about a win-win and doing things intelligently.

The beautiful thing about this approach is that it is extremely sustainable, even through a high volume cycling season!

Yes, the sets and repetitions per set will change a little bit, in order to take into account the fatigue you'll most likely be carrying from your riding, but it would not change much.

Here's an example of what an in-season hypertrophy block may look like, progressing from the sample above:

- For week 1, we'll do 2 sets of 10 repetitions, at an RPE 6

- For week 2, we'll do 2 sets of 10 repetitions, at an RPE 7

- Week 3 will be 2 sets of 12 repetitions, at an RPE 7

- Week 4 will be 2 sets of 8 repetitions. at an RPE 7

Once again, we aren't looking at a huge change week to week, except in the RPE from weeks 1 to week 2, and in the total volume of work done from week to week, simply by adding 2 reps, or a higher RPE.

It is important to note again here, that your RPE will determine the weight, as RPE and RIR (Reps in Reserve) will allow you to self-regulate based on the amount of fatigue you're carrying on that day, at that time, for that particular exercise.

Because we are not Olympic weightlifters or Power lifters, the amount of weight on the bar is of no importance to you. Only the stress we place on the organism (that's you), for its current abilities.

But There's A Catch...

The above looks really simple, and easy to put in to practice, but there is a really important catch, or "Lynchpin," as Seth Godin likes to say, as this detail really makes the entire strength training program work well:

You have to change the exercise every Mesocycle.

If you keep the same exercise, but only change the sets and reps as we did in our example, you won't get the results you're after, as the body adapts to a given training stimulus.

So you cannot just keep doing front squats and change the sets and reps. You need to also make some kind of change to the exercise itself. Otherwise, the training adaptations will fall off. To date, research has suggested this happens between weeks 5-8, with week 6 being the most common number thrown around.

However, it is important to note that the participants in the study were mostly general fitness and health strength trainees. I've found for some cyclists (and triathletes), it can actually be very beneficial to keep exercises for up to 8 weeks, as they both appreciate the 2 weeks to learn how to do the movement better, and not having to tackle learning all new movements every month as it just takes more time. The choice of whether to change the exercises every 4, 6, or 8 weeks is up to you.

But don't keep the same exercises beyond 8 weeks.

The Expert's "Lynchpin"

You may be thinking *"Uh oh, I don't know that many exercises! How am I supposed to change it up every 4-8 weeks?!?"*

Well, here's an expert insight that I've been told is worth the price of admission just to learn this one thing:

It does not need to be a fully new movement. You just have to modify the exercise a little!

This is where something as simple as performing a Box Squat instead of a normal squat can be that change... or perhaps you use a 2-1-1-1 Tempo (Tempo was covered in Chapter 4) instead of being self-paced.

The slight changes make the exercise a little different, and thus the demand changes. Kinda like when instead of just giving you a Lactate Threshold Interval at a % of your FTP, I give you a cadence range to go with it.

Same interval, more suffering.

You're welcome, by the way.

Those little cadence changes in your cycling plan also help drive some nice improvements in your neurological system, and can really help you produce more power over longer Lactate Threshold intervals.

Organizing Your Training Week: Balancing Strength Training and Cycling Workouts

Striking a balance between strength training and cycling-specific workouts is key to prevent over-training and optimize recovery, and more importantly, driving adaptations. This means, as we've discussed so far, that you're not smashing yourself to bits in the weight room, leaving any set of stairs appearing like Freddy Krueger to you afterwards and for the next few days.

It also means that we want to find a way to blend your strength training with your on-bike training in a way that we are creating an upwards vortex of fitness and progression (thus the name of my company, Human Vortex Training).

Current research, as of the end of 2023, has suggested that 4-6 hours between strength training and endurance activities is optimal, with some stating as long as 9 hours if you want to perform both on the same day.

I wish there was some magical formula I could share with you that will give you all the gains from your strength + cycling training, but the truth is that when it comes to results, the most important thing is to find the recipe that works best for you.

Some find great success by riding in the morning, and then doing strength training either at lunchtime or in the late afternoon.

Others have found sound results by strength training on the 2-3 days a week they are not riding (but leaving one day completely off to rest).

But I've got to tell you, purely in my own experience with those whom I've coached when we are looking to improve on-bike performance with the inclusion of strength training, the best results have come when the trainings are either separated by as little time as possible (a quick shower and small meal = around 60-90 minutes), or by around 3-4 hours, but not much more.

This started off with busy professionals and parents coming to do their strength training sessions with me mid-morning, after they finished their morning rides, dropped their kids off at school or took care of early meetings/emails, and came for a strength session. They almost all wanted the time window of 60-120 minutes after they got off the bike.

Oh, and an important detail here, the cycling workouts are ***always*** first... and we are doing strength training after the shorter (90-120 min) high-intensity interval rides, but not after long endurance rides.

This recipe, which I have been trying to disprove for over a decade, keeps on rising to the top, despite several riders insisting on *"following the current research"* and splitting their training on the days so that riding and strength are separated by 8-9 hours.

To me, at least, this makes sense, and may be worth noting that while splitting your strength and riding into opposite ends of the day may *seem* ideal, it can have negative effects on your ability to fall asleep and the quality of your sleep. This is due to your body needing 2-4 hours for the body's systems to dip back to baseline/resting.

With the cards already stacked against you and your ability to catch full night of quality Z's thanks to your hormonal status changing (both men and women), as well as the need to get up and pee more throughout the night, working out anywhere past the late afternoon hours may just not make sense for you, due to its trickle-down effects that can pull the rug out from your best efforts.

What we've also found (and made total sense from the get-go) is that performing strength training on the same day as an endurance building ride leaves you with very poor results on both sides of the coin. This jibes completely with the fact that these are two competing adaptations to physical stressors. With the research done so far on mTOR and the so-called *"interference effect,"* this seems to explain that phenomenon.

Needless to say, aside from a post-long endurance ride movement session aimed at counterbalancing the hours in the ride position with a focus on breathwork to kick start the recovery & adaptation process, I am strongly against doing an endurance ride (or a ride aimed at improving your ability to ride for longer periods of time) followed by a strength-building session.

Give your body one stimulus and let it run with it when working at the extreme ends of the spectrum of building either strength at one end, and endurance at the other.

Now, if you are going through a 5-10 day "training load bomb" (aka Training Camp") is a special exception, where we will probably let strength slide a bit, replacing what we've discussed here about lifting heavy sh*t, with a focus on dynamic movements and proximal stiffness training which are short, focused, and done at a time they will help drive better adaptations to your riding.

But once training camp is over, we're right back to a consistent strength program.

Aside from what appears to be a hard and fast rule of "don't try to program your body for extreme opposites of strength and endurance on the same day, the only correct answer to the question of *"Where do I put my strength training?"* is to put them wherever you will be able to be consistent with them, and what works best for you.

While the approaches you use may transform or progress over time, if you pay attention to what your body is telling you, water it, get quality sleep consistently, and show up to your strength sessions regularly to do the best you can on that day, at that time, you are certainly going to see success.

Should I Lift Before Or After Riding?

This leads to one of the most common questions for those cyclists who find it easier to put their strength and riding sessions together: Which should I do first?

As I laid out before, I've had an overwhelming majority- but not all!- riders I've worked with, who have found that doing their interval sessions before their lift and having a short 30-90 minute shower + food break in between, has worked extremely well for them.

However, the answer to the question is highly personal, as it is really best to do what works best for you. Give one way a try for a full 4 weeks and keep track of how you feel as well as the results you see. Then do the opposite, keeping track of those.

Which felt better to you?

Which was easier for you?

Which gave you better results?

Go with that one... until you either feel you need a change, or see that it is no longer working well for you.

Important Early Morning Strength & After Riding Strength Pointers

If you are going to lift before your riding first thing in the morning, it would be incredibly wise to perform the cow-camel exercise for a singular set of 10-12 gentle repetitions.

Reason being, that when we sleep, our intervertebral discs fill with fluid, essentially replacing the fluid that was lost through yesterday.

But our discs don't just fill to the same level, they actually overfill a little, leaving our discs a little more plump than usual. We naturally push these fluids out when we first get up and walk around in the morning. But if you're going to go strength train after rolling out of bed first thing, it's best practice to use the cow-camel exercise to help move this extra fluid out.

It is also best practice to perform the cow-camel exercise before riding first thing in the morning as well, but I'll leave that up to you.

If you'll be riding first and then strength training shortly thereafter, you'll want to have either the *McGill Crunch* (performed correctly) or the *Shielded Breath* exercise, as well as a *Side Plank Top Foot Forward* and *Bird-Dog* variation in the exercises of your pre-strength dynamic warm-up.

Reason being that after riding the bike in a flexed forward position, your ability to properly fire up your core (everything between your neck, elbows, and knees) to produce an appropriate spinal brace, will be decreased.

These 3 exercises, often called "***The McGill Big 3,***" will help to set the table to protect your spine and build proximal stiffness, so that you can create strong and powerful movements through your shoulders and hips.

You can find a playlist of these exercises on the HV Training YouTube Channel, for free, titled "The McGill Big 3."

Building Your Training Week

Perhaps one of the biggest misunderstandings about training is that many feel that it needs to be high intensity all the time to be beneficial. But this is mistaken, especially for your strength training.

When we begin to look at your training months (Mesocycles) and weeks (Microcycles) we must understand that you cannot go hard all the time. It will simply fry you, especially if you're over the age of 40.

While we do need to go intense at times in order to drive the adaptations we are after, we actually use the lower intensity days and times in order to help improve those very adaptations.

This is where strength training, when you understand it and implement it correctly, or just well, masters cyclists absolutely massive rewards in-season!

Here are the 3 different kinds of strength training days that you should be considering.

Development Training Session

What often comes to mind when we think about strength training, the Development Training Session is a hard session, usually ending with an overall RPE of 8 or 9.

I never recommend going to an RPE 10 for a strength training session for any of my sport-athletes! You are in the weight room to get stronger for your sport, not for strength's sake!

Going to an RPE 10 where you are fearing the stairs or slinking your way out of the gym, means that you've now derailed all of your body's resources from improving from the session and your riding, to needing to hit the emergency button and push all resources to repair the massive amount of damage you've done to your muscles.

It is important to understand that development sessions are far more about the *specific* exercises you are doing with a push to improve performance.

This can mean that there is one main exercise, let's say a Hex Bar Deadlift off of Blocks, where you are either working on the edge of your ability to maintain great technique with a weight or resistance that has you at an RPE 8-9 the last repetition or two. It is the traditional "Lift heavy sh*t" mentality for that main, _singular_ exercise. But not for every single exercise in that days program.

The development session will leave you feeling it the next day, and every now and again, possibly the 2nd day after. . . but that is **not** our goal. Our goal is to get the work we need on that main exercise, with great technique, and the correct weight and RPE, so that you get the desired adaptation from your training.

For many masters riders, one development session every 7-10 days will give you the results you're looking for, but it does depend on your ability to recover and adapt.

A Sample Development Training Session

Let's take a look at a sample Development Training Session.

Note that A's, B's, and C's are to be done in pairs, one right after the other (A1. Right into A2. etc.), with the rest clock starting after completion of the 2nd exercise.

Dynamic Warmup

1-2 Breathing exercises

2-4 Dynamic warmups

Main Lift

A1. Hex Bar Deadlift off Blocks
1*10 Warm-up, 1*8 RPE 7, 1*5 RPE 7, 1*3 RPE 8

A2. Box Jumps w/ quiet landing (to 18in box) 3*5

B1. Seated D-Grip Alternating Rows 2*10/ side RPE 7

B2. Half Kneeling 1-arm KB Shoulder Press w/ Opposite Hand Reach 2*10/ side RPE 6-7

C1. Suitcase Carries 3*20 sec RPE 7

C2. Stability Ball Stir The Pot 3*5 ea way

D. Crocodile Breathing - 3 minutes straight, Box Breathing Style

5 min soft tissue work if/as needed, not for pain, but a quick roll to push fluids.

Stimulation Training Session

The Stimulation Training Session is where many of us will find the big wins. Yes, of course we need development sessions as well, but strength training is much more about consistency, than it is about tenacity.

Stimulation sessions will make up roughly 70-80% of most programs, as these sessions are more easy for us to recover and adapt from.

But be advised!

Stimulation days can, and in my opinion should, also have some challenging lifting in them when appropriate!

Stimulation sessions are the strength training sessions where we hit an RPE of 6-7 for the session as a whole, but there can be a focal exercise where we are hitting an RPE of 8 on the last set.

The stimulation training session is more about the managing of load and staying within your abilities to recover and adapt by the next day than it is about just punching the clock, although there are certainly days where they are just that.

A Sample Stimulation Training Session

Let's take a look at a sample Stimulation Training Session, using the same exercises as above, so you can easily understand the difference.

Same rule applies to the groupings (A's, B's, C's).

Dynamic Warmup

1-2 Breathing exercises

2-4 Dynamic warmups

Main Lift

A1. Hex Bar Deadlift off Blocks 3*8 RPE 7
- *Keep midsection braced, Focus on Push the floor away w/ Hips and Shoulders rising together.*

A2. Box Jumps w/ quiet landing (to 18in box) 3*5
- *Focus on getting full hip extension off floor*

B1. Seated D-Grip Alternating Rows 2*10/ side RPE 6
- *Focus on technique and posture*

B2. Half Kneeling 1-arm KB Shoulder Press w/ Opposite Hand Reach 2*10/ side RPE 6-7

C1. Suitcase Carries 3*30 sec RPE 7

C2. Stability Ball Stir The Pot 3*5 ea way
- Focus on Keeping midsection braced, move only from shoulder blades

D. Crocodile Breathing - 3 minutes straight, Box Breathing Style

5 min soft tissue work if/as needed, not for pain, but a quick roll to push fluids.

This may look really similar to the Development day, but there are some pretty big differences!

1. The Hex bar Deadlifts are straight sets of 8 at an RPE of 7, with a focus on a technique cue. This, for most cyclists, will often lead to weights increasing a little from set to set, but overall staying pretty much the same, as you aim to refine that technique focal point, not just pick up heavy stuff.

2. Cue for Jumps changes the focus from intensity, to quality.

3. Lower RPE and a focus on technique and posture for the seated rows. This doesn't look like much on paper, but it often means lower weight and much higher movement quality.

4. The Suitcase carries for a longer time. While they are at the same RPE, the length of time will require a lighter weight.

To make it crystal clear here:

The big difference between the Development Session and the Stimulation Session is the time of recovery and adaptation. The Development Session had increasingly heavier loads for the deadlifts, and repetition ranges and RPE's that encourage or allow for heavier loads or resistance to be used.

The Stimulation Session may have similar RPE's, but due to the straight sets and focus on technique, the weights and resistance will be lighter.

Of course there will be cues on our development day, we do of course want as high quality as possible, but we limit it to one, maybe two things that we've been working on for that rider, which will help them succeed with the heavier weights/ higher RPE.

High Performance Recovery Training Session

Perhaps one of the biggest lessons learned through my nearly 20 years of working as a strength coach for endurance athletes, is that strength training can, and should be, used as a recovery method.

This may seem counterintuitive, but it actually makes total sense once you understand the stresses we place on our bodies by riding our bikes, and what the body requires in order to recover.

These recovery sessions are an absolutely fantastic tool to help you keep fresh during a long season, as well as to keep your body moving well.

Recovery Training sessions are usually fairly short, 20-40 minutes, and include breathing drills, corrective exercises, targeted movement drills, and concentric-only lifts, finishing with breathing and soft tissue work. In these sessions, we do not go heavy on our strength, but we do move some weight.

One of the big keys to the success of these recovery sessions is making sure to get the breathwork and soft tissue work at the end of this (and really every) workout.

The Concentric-only lifts I have found to be useful are Drop-Deadlifts (with the bar up off the floor 6 inches or higher) and Anderson Squats (for cyclists I've found putting the pins/rack where you start from your ¾ squat position are best).

For Anderson Squats, you MUST have long pins or racks to take the bar from. Trying to use the hooks that normally hold the barbell for our sets is not only a fool's errand, but also extremely dangerous. Anderson Squats are best done either in what is referred to as a *"cage"* or *"squat rig"* where you are inside a steel U frame, with the pins or racks running between both sides of the U, or off of Power Racks, which are long arms, designed for this kind of work.

A Sample High Performance Recovery Training Session

Recovery Training Sessions have a very different flow than our Stimulation and Development days, as we are truly putting all the focus on lifting stuff, but making sure you leave the session feeling better than you came in, and driving positive training adaptations for both your riding, and strength training.

These sessions are dialed in to what that individual needs, but follows the following recipe:

1. **Breathing Exercise** - aimed to destress the autonomic nervous system, as well as continue to work on the ability to breathe.

2. **Mobility work** - We use 2-3 dynamic mobility exercises to help hit high-return areas for that individual.

3. **Movement** - some kind of light strength exercises to increase deep tissue blood flow, especially for high-value target areas or movement patterns, limiting eccentric loading.

4. **Strength** - Concentric only lifts such as Concentric-only Deadlifts, Anderson Squats, or Kettlebell swings. Just enough to fire up the nervous system, with your energy increasing. Think along the lines of 2-3 sets of 4-6 repetitions.

   This part of the session can, and often is, relatively heavy! But we do these in a way that it is firing you up, allowing you to see improvements in your status, not feeling more tired.

5. **Breathing** - this time around to help drive your heart rate down as close to resting HR as possible, and begin to dial down your internal hormonal environment to kick-start your recovery and adaptation.

6. **Targeted Static Stretching, or soft tissue work** - For some, but not all of my masters athletes, we add in 3-5 minutes of static stretching or targeted soft tissue work here. This not only adds to your leaving the session feeling much better, but also helps reinforce the act of doing the complete HPRT session, as all together you'll feel much better and move better.

I cannot stress this enough, these High Performance Recovery Training Sessions are incredibly valuable, when done correctly.

These sessions are incredibly valuable, especially as a masters rider looking to improve posture, mobility, bone health, and to feel great on the bike. Not only do they help you keep up your strength training, but they actually drive up and forward your adaptations for your riding and *from* your riding.

Sample Strength Training Week: A Blueprint for Cycling Success

Let's take a look at the two most useful training week loading strategies that we can use for masters cyclists (and triathletes).

Beginner Strength Training Week

As we get into strength training, there is a need to slowly increase the stress on the system (that's you and your body) so that we are allowing enough time for the body to recover and adapt to the training stimulus.

For that reason, as a beginner, we will be starting your strength training week off with a High Performance Recovery Training Session.

These sessions, as noted above, allow you to recover and adapt faster to your weekend training loads, which are usually some of our highest of the week. It may not look like much, but performing an HPRT session on Monday does wonders for your training week!

Here's how it would look for a beginner:

Option #1 - 3 Days per week, beginner

Monday - High Performance Recovery Training

Tuesday -Stimulation

Wednesday - No Strength

Thursday - Stimulation

Friday - No Strength

Saturday - No Strength

Sunday- No Strength

Option #2 - 4 Days per week, Beginner

Monday - High Performance Recovery Training

Tuesday - Stimulation

Wednesday - No Strength

Thursday - Stimulation

Friday - High Performance Recovery Training

Saturday - No Strength

Sunday- No Strength

You'll certainly notice that as a beginner we do not have a development session. This is due in large part to the fact that there is not really a need! Remember those *"newbie gains"* we talked about earlier?

And remember what Anatoliy Bondarchuk said about losing the adaptations 2x? As a beginner, just by showing up and putting in quality work, you will see improvements. Your ego may tell you that you need a development day, but you do not need one as a beginner to consistent strength training. You'll only be burning energy and time.

Now let's take a look at what an intermediate program would look like.

Intermediate Strength Training Week

As you move to an intermediate level, usually at year 2 or 3, depending on your movement capabilities and how you managed the trainings due to life and stress, the HPRT sessions will be used as either a primer before the weekend (this example on Friday), or to replace Monday's stimulation training on the weeks you realize that you bit off a more than you could chew over the weekend, or due to a big event or race that you just had.

Here is what an intermediate week would look like:

Option #1 - 3 Days per week, Intermediate

Monday - Stimulation

Tuesday - Development

Wednesday - No Strength

Thursday - Stimulation

Friday - No Strength

Saturday - No Strength

Sunday- No Strength

Option #2 - 4 Days per week, Intermediate

Monday - Stimulation

Tuesday - Development

Wednesday - No Strength

Thursday - Stimulation

Friday - High Performance Recovery Training

Saturday - No Strength

Sunday- No Strength

Advanced Strength Training Week

By the time you get to the advanced strength training stage, you'll have been strength training consistently, year-round, for anywhere between 3-5+ years.

Yes, really, that long.

With cycling being our main focus for you, we allow more time for the strength to build it's critical mass, before pushing you up a level. Of course, this is by far no set rule, as it truly depends on you, your stage in life, your ability to recover from your trainings, and your goals.

In all honesty, I still have a few riders who have been strength training with me for over 6 years, and they are still at the Intermediate level. This is both their choice, as they feel much better following those ramp rates and loads, as well as their body dictating what they can and cannot do.

It's your job, as a responsible adult, to keep your ego in check, and allow yourself to stay at the level which allows you to continually build fitness and strength by staying healthy, moving better than before, and to recover and adapt quickly, deeply, and fully.

Let's take a look at what an advance strength training program might look like:

Option #1 - 3 days per week, Advanced

Monday - Stimulation

Tuesday - Development

Wednesday - No Strength

Thursday - Stimulation

Friday - No Strength

Saturday - No Strength

Sunday- No Strength

Option #2 - 4 days per week, Intermediate

Monday - Stimulation

Tuesday - Development

Wednesday - No Strength

Thursday - Stimulation or Development

Friday - High Performance Recovery Training

Saturday - No Strength

You'll notice that the 3-day per week program has no difference in it. That is just what I have found works over the last 15+ years working with cyclists and triathletes. Perhaps in another 15 years that will change.

The only noticeable difference is in the 4-day per week program, where the Thursday session can be Stimulation or Development. This will depend mostly upon the riders needs, time of training year, as well as how well they are adapting. 80-90% of the time, we will do a second Stimulation Session. This is due to our playing the long game with the strength training programming. That said, there are some occasions, often for a very brief point in time, where we may add a second development session.

But you need to be very careful about doing this, and I do not recommend doing 2 development sessions a week for more than 3 weeks in a row, without a proper deload from both strength and riding.

Energy and time are two resources we cannot get back, and especially as an endurance sport athlete (or rider, if your prefer), who wants to be feeling and moving well on the bike, there is more to lose than win by pushing hard in the gym that many weeks in a row.

I don't even do that with my pro basketball guys, who are some strong dudes, as when we take a step back and look at the big picture, there is almost always something better we can spend your time and energy on

That said, if you want to push hard for 2-3 weeks like that, make sure you deload both riding and strength for the 3rd or 4th week, allowing full recovery and adaptation. This does not mean a week of low-level endurance rides and strength!

2-3 HPRT sessions and a stimulation session are a good idea, as is a singular short, sharp session on the bike.

An important note for the Advanced 3 day program, is that should there be a 4th day which comes available, we would only add an HRPT session to Friday. That's it.

There is no need to do another development day, as the rider is only used to a 3 day a week strength load, and adding another development day is very likely to shove you off a cliff.

Think about Wile E. Coyote chasing Road Runner, but he runs out of ground below him, only to plummet to the canyon floor below, with that ever- hilarious riding ring of dust or smoke...

It's pretty much the same.

Seriously.

You do the development session, and only 2-4 days later that you have "messed up". And the ground runs out, as you either get sick, are too sore to train on the bike with any kind of quality, have energy drops, trouble sleeping, or a whole host of other issues.

I can assure you, it may be funny to read this and think about it like Wile E., but it sure as heck is not funny when it happens to you!

Why No Recommendations On How To Set Up My Week With Rides And Strength?

As I outlined above in "*Organizing Your Training Week: Balancing Strength Training & Cycling Workouts*" there is no simple answer.

Nor is there one template I can share with you.

There are so many variables that come into play when building a riding + strength training week, that I cannot, in good conscience, write a sample here.

Yes, I know this is disappointing.

But it's simply the right answer:

It depends.

And without getting to know you:

- Your ride and strength history

- Current limitations

- Current strengths

- Time available to dedicate to each discipline

- Your upcoming goals

- Your Current movement abilities

- Your ability to recover and adapt from your riding and strength training

It just is not right to paint in very broad strokes, which would lead so many down a path to disappointment, wasted time & energy, or far worse.

In conclusion, tailoring your training plan is a critical step in optimizing your cycling performance. By crafting a personalized strength training program that aligns with your goals and capabilities, organizing your training week effectively, and incorporating a strength training program specifically tailored to cycling objectives and movement capabilities, you can maximize your potential on the bike. Emphasizing proper form and technique, and considering periodization principles will further enhance your progress and help you reach new levels of performance as well as a higher quality of life off the bike, and help significantly stack the longevity cards in favor of a life filled with vitality, energy, and the ability to enjoy every day with movement and strength.

Chapter Nine

Observations Regarding Longevity

In this chapter, we will take a look at lifestyle factors and habits that contribute to a long and active life beyond the physical realm of exercise and healthy eating. While these aspects are crucial for maintaining physical well-being, there are other dimensions of our daily routines that play a significant role in promoting longevity and overall wellness.

Exploring Life Beyond the Gym and the Bike

Longevity is not solely dependent on physical fitness; it encompasses a holistic approach to wellness. We must delve deeper into our daily habits, stress management techniques, social connections, attitude towards aging, cognitive stimulation, relationships with food, regular health check-ups, and staying active mentally and physically to unravel the secrets of a longer and more fulfilling life.

1. Prioritize Sleep:

Adequate sleep is crucial for overall health and longevity. During sleep, our bodies engage in essential repair and rejuvenation processes, optimizing immune function, hormone regulation, and cognitive processes. Research indicates that individuals who consistently get a good night's sleep tend to have a lower risk of chronic diseases such as heart disease, diabetes, and obesity. To prioritize sleep, create a sleep routine by maintaining consistent sleep and wake times, establishing a comfortable sleep environment, and practicing relaxation techniques like meditation or reading before bed.

2. Stress Management:

Chronic stress can take a toll on our physical and mental well-being, ultimately impacting our longevity. Ongoing stress contributes to conditions such as high blood pressure, cardiovascular disease, and cognitive decline. To effectively manage stress, explore various techniques such as meditation, deep breathing exercises, or engaging in activities that bring you joy and relaxation, like hobbies or spending time in nature. Cultivate mindfulness by being present, and develop strategies to reduce stress in your daily life, such as proper time management and setting realistic expectations.

3. Social Connections:

Maintaining strong social connections and engaging in meaningful relationships is vital for our overall well-being. Research suggests that individuals with robust social networks tend to live longer and have better health outcomes. Social interactions provide emotional support, reduce feelings of loneliness, and promote a sense of purpose and belonging. Cultivate relationships with friends, family, and community members, and actively participate in social activities and events that bring you joy and foster positive social connections. Join clubs, volunteer, or engage in group activities that align with your interests.

4. Embrace a Positive Attitude:

Keeping a positive outlook and mindset can have a profound impact on our health and longevity. Studies have indicated that individuals with a positive attitude towards aging tend to live longer and maintain better cognitive function. Cultivate a positive attitude by practicing gratitude, focusing on the present moment, and surrounding yourself with positivity. Engage in activities that make you happy, pursue hobbies that bring you joy, and nourish your mental well-being. Find ways to reframe negative thoughts and cultivate an optimistic perspective on life.

5. Cognitive Stimulation:

Engaging in activities that stimulate the mind can help maintain cognitive function and reduce the risk of age-related cognitive decline. Challenge your brain by participating in intellectually stimulating activities such as puzzles, reading, learning new skills, or engaging in stimulating conversations. Consider trying new hobbies or taking up educational courses to constantly challenge and exercise your mental faculties. Stay curious and open-minded, as lifelong learning promotes brain plasticity and cognitive vitality.

6. Healthy Relationships with Food:

Following a balanced and nutritious diet is crucial for longevity. Focus on consuming whole foods that are rich in essential nutrients, including fruits, vegetables, lean proteins, and healthy fats. Be mindful of portion sizes and avoid excessive consumption of processed foods, sugary drinks, and unhealthy fats. Cultivate a healthy relationship with food by listening to your body's hunger and fullness cues, practicing mindful eating, and indulging in moderation. Avoid restrictive diets that can be detrimental to your long-term health and instead focus on nourishing your body with wholesome, nutrient-dense foods. Consult a healthcare professional or registered dietitian for personalized guidance.

7. Regular Health Check-ups:

Regular health check-ups and screenings are essential for early detection and prevention of health conditions. Staying proactive about your health by scheduling routine check-ups, dental visits, and age-appropriate screenings can help identify potential issues before they escalate. Address any health concerns promptly, as early intervention often leads to more successful outcomes. Don't neglect preventative care, as it plays a pivotal role in maintaining good health and longevity. Maintain open communication with your healthcare provider and follow their recommendations.

8. Stay Active Mentally and Physically:

Engaging in regular physical exercise helps maintain strength, flexibility, cardiovascular health, and overall well-being. Incorporate a combination of strength training, cardiovascular exercise, and flexibility work into your routine to reap the benefits of a well-rounded fitness regimen. Experiment with different activities to find what you enjoy most, whether it's dancing, swimming, hiking, or practicing yoga. Additionally, stimulate your mind by participating in activities that promote mental agility, such as reading, solving puzzles, learning new languages, or playing musical instruments. Engaging in mental and physical activities not only keeps your body strong but also enhances cognitive function, boosts mood, and promotes lifelong learning.

By incorporating these longevity hacks into your daily routine, you can enhance your overall well-being and increase your chances of living a vibrant, active, and fulfilling life for years to come. Remember, longevity extends far beyond the walls of the gym and the pedals of a bike. Embrace these holistic lifestyle factors and embark on a journey towards a long and flourishing existence.

Chapter Ten

Beyond The Gains

Quality Living

Reflecting on how intelligent strength training transcends physical benefits, enhancing the overall quality of life for the masters cyclist, we delve deeper into the profound impact it can have on various aspects of our existence. While the physical gains are undoubtedly important and evident to anyone observing our muscular strides and enhanced endurance, it is essential to understand the broader benefits that extend far beyond mere physical attributes.

First and foremost, let's explore the mental and cognitive aspects that come into play when masters cyclists engage in intelligent strength training. The discipline, focus, and determination required in our training can spill over into other areas of our lives, leading to increased productivity, resilience, and a profound sense of accomplishment. As we push ourselves to our limits on the bike, we develop mental fortitude that transcends mere physical prowess, translating into everyday challenges and obstacles we face off the saddle. Such mental resilience empowers us to strive for personal growth and success with unwavering determination, breaking through barriers that might have once seemed insurmountable. This mental strength becomes a guiding force, propelling us forward in our careers, relationships, and personal endeavors, ultimately equipping us with the tools to conquer the most formidable hurdles life throws our way.

Moreover, strength training offers a unique opportunity for self-reflection and self-improvement. As we engage in the process of challenging ourselves physically, we concurrently embark on a journey of self-discovery and self-awareness. By understanding our bodies - identifying our strengths and weaknesses - and actively working to improve, we gain a deeper understanding of ourselves as individuals. This process fosters a sense of self-confidence and self-worth that spills over into all aspects of our lives, enhancing our relationships, careers, and personal fulfillment. As we refine our physical capabilities, we also refine our understanding of who we are at our core, cultivating an unshakable belief in our potential and capabilities.

However, quality living is not solely rooted in personal development; it also lies in achieving harmony and balance in our lives. Intelligent strength training serves as an invaluable teacher, emphasizing the significance of listening to our bodies and prioritizing rest and recovery. By understanding the value of restorative practices such as proper nutrition, adequate sleep, and stress management, we can optimize our physical and mental well-being. This holistic approach to living allows us to show up fully in every aspect of our lives, whether it is spending quality time with our loved ones, pursuing our careers with vigor and passion, or exploring other interests and hobbies. The intelligent masters cyclist understands that a life well-lived requires nourishment and rejuvenation, for it is during these breaks that the seeds of inspiration and creativity are sown, propelling us forward even more effectively when we once again don our cycling gear.

Beyond personal development and balance, strength training provides masters cyclists with a means to embrace the joy of movement and self-expression. As we become stronger and more agile, we gain a newfound freedom and confidence in our bodies. The physical capabilities we develop through strength training open doors to new experiences and opportunities, pushing our boundaries and expanding our horizons. Whether it's conquering challenging mountain climbs that were once deemed impossible, participating in epic cycling adventures that push our limits, or engaging in other physical activities that ignite our passions, we can fully immerse ourselves in the present moment, savoring every sensation and relishing in the exhilaration of being alive. This boundless energy and zest for life serve as a constant reminder that with strength comes the power to make the most of every moment.

Furthermore, intelligent strength training fosters resilience in the face of adversity, both on and off the bike. Masters cyclists face numerous challenges, from injuries and setbacks to the mental struggles of pushing through physical barriers. Through consistent and intelligent training, we develop a mindset that embraces challenges as opportunities for growth and learning. The ability to overcome obstacles with determination and tenacity translates into a resilience that extends far beyond the realms of cycling. In our personal and professional lives, we become equipped to handle setbacks, adapt to change, and bounce back from failures with a renewed sense of purpose and resilience. This resilience becomes the foundation from which we build a life filled with confidence, perseverance, and the capacity to overcome any hurdle that comes our way.

Finally, this chapter emphasizes the importance of fostering a supportive community. By surrounding ourselves with like-minded individuals who share our passion for intelligent strength training and cycling, we create a network of support and encouragement that further enriches the overall quality of our lives. Engaging with others who understand our journey and can relate to our challenges and triumphs not only provides a sense of camaraderie, but also instills a sense of accountability and inspiration. This supportive community becomes a haven where we can share our knowledge, experiences, and aspirations, propelling one another to new heights and fostering an environment where everyone thrives and grows together. The collective energy of such a community becomes an unstoppable force, propelling the master's cyclist towards continuous growth and success in all aspects of their lives.

As we conclude this book, let us reflect on the profound impact intelligent strength training can have on enhancing the overall quality of life for masters cyclists. Beyond the physical gains, mental resilience, personal development, harmony, self-expression, and a supportive community all contribute to a life lived to its fullest potential. Let us forge ahead, continue to push our limits, and live a life fueled by strength, passion, and purpose, inspiring others along the way.

Chapter Eleven

Why You Should Consider A Coach

Coaching, in its modern format, has been around since the late 1990s. People still think of it as something new, but in reality, coaching has been around for millennia. There has never been a period in the history of humanity where coaches did not exist.

Sure, it might have looked a little different, but coaching is as old as the hills. Modern day coaching may be more refined and a lot more commercially viable, but the principles remain the same.

What Does a Coach Do?

Coaches have the skills and knowledge to advise, support, and encourage their clients.

They help them to:

- Make sound decisions

- Take effective actions

- Resolve their challenges in the most efficient way possible

- Learn from the process, so they can repeat it whenever they want

- A coach also has the ability to remain detached from the issues at hand.

Consider the wise words of Albert Einstein:

"We cannot solve our problems with the same thinking we used when we created them."

Time Is Money

In the modern era, in life and business, time is money. There's an ever-increasing amount of cooperation and collaboration going on both in businesses and in people's private lives. We need to figure things out almost on the fly these days while dealing with different time zones and cultures.

Everyone has their own unique issues to handle alongside everything else that needs to be accommodated, and then there's the technology we all use to connect with everybody and everything.

Life is definitely more complex today, and it certainly seems to speed up every time you turn around. It doesn't take long before we begin to have thoughts of overwhelm and burnout in our minds.

The question we need to ask ourselves is this: *"How long can I justify spending time and money on this issue trying to figure it out for myself, knowing what Albert Einstein said about problem solving?"*

If having a coach could save you time and money, it would be ridiculous NOT to hire one, wouldn't it?

Throughout history, every King has had an Advisor (Coach) in every culture. Every military leader has had a Strategist (Coach), every World Class Athlete has had a trainer (Coach), and every Entertainer has had a Manager (Coach).

Who Hires a Coach?

The only conclusion we can draw from the history of coaching is that **the people who hire a coach fall into two camps**:

- People who are at the top of their game and want to stay there, or

- People who aspire to be at the top of their game and want to get there as fast as they can

Many people will say that they want to change themselves, their life, their job, or their circumstances, but in real terms, they are fearful of change. They delay, procrastinate, and make excuses. They lack self-confidence and the drive to follow through. It's human nature. It's what ordinary people always do.

People who hire a Coach are not ordinary people.

They are inspired and have vision. They embrace change and are prepared to get fully engaged in making positive changes in their life. Plus, they don't want it to take forever!

They have a sense of urgency, and they want someone they can lean on, confide in, use as a sounding board, and rely on to help them make the inevitable tough decisions that they can see on the horizon.

People hiring their first coach are often racked with pessimism. They think, *"What if I waste my money?"*

Consider that, before you hire a coach, you're already wasting time, which is the same as money, and you lack the resources to resolve the issues at hand. It would cost you less to hire a coach and find out first-hand and NOW how unbelievably useful a coach can be.

People who are hiring their second or subsequent coach have no pessimism. What they are looking for is the perfect fit for them and the circumstances they find themselves in.

Within reason, money is not the issue and they never think about the possibility of wasting it. Their main concern is finding the RIGHT coach and then hoping that the coach they choose has a spot left open where they can be accommodated, and can they start today?

Is Hiring a Coach Right For You?

Maybe. Maybe not.

- Are you at a point where NOT taking action is costing you time and money?

- Do you feel stuck in your struggles?

- Could you use encouragement and sage advice in moving forward?

If you answered *"yes"* to any of these questions, perhaps a coach can get you moving in the right direction to help you create the life you desire - and sooner rather than later.

If hiring a coach seems right for you, or you're not sure if hiring a coach is the best path for you, feel free to schedule a no obligation Clarity Call with me at https://calendly.com/humanvortextraining/30min. I'll help you determine if it's the right decision for you. No risk, no obligation. Just me helping you determine your best course of action.

Chapter Twelve

What To Do Next

Here's How To Get Started Lifting Heavy While Adding Longevity And Quality To Your Life...

The next step for you is simple:

Get started!

Taking action is your immediate step. Nothing happens until you make it happen. You now have everything you need to add health and fitness into your life.

Still not sure of where to start, or exactly what to do?

I'm more than happy to help you get everything in place, and get you that healthy and fit body.

If you'd like me to help, reach out to me by scheduling a no obligation Clarity Call with me at https://calendly.com/humanvortextraining/30min. If you enjoyed this book, you'll do even better with me leading the way.

I'm good at what I do, just like you're good at what you do.

Instead of trying to figure everything out yourself, let me help you dial in your new health and nutrition program. I help folks just like you find the time to add health and fitness into their lives. And stick to it.

Step 1: We spend time together outlining and developing your training program, nutrition, and overall strategy to fully dial in the perfect solution for you and the time you have.

Step 2: We begin integrating your training and nutrition habits into your busy schedule.

Step 3: We dial everything in from your training to your nutrition to make adding more healthy habits into your busy life a walk in the park.

Step 4: Once we have your habits down pat, we monitor everything to ensure everything is working seamlessly to get you the greatest results in the shortest time.

Most people think it takes years of hard work and countless hours of meal prep to get or stay healthy and fit.

Truth is, my done-with-you program is designed to make it an easy and stress-free transition for you, so we give you everything you need to ensure your success in the shortest possible time.

If you're ready to add a fitness program into your life that gets twice the results in half the time, let's get on the phone for a short call with me by scheduling a no obligation Clarity Call with me at https://calendly.com/humanvortextraining/30min.

About the Author

Who is Menachem Brodie?

Menachem Brodie is an international best-selling author, podcaster, and strength coach who has helped masters athletes of all backgrounds, from those in their mid-30's all the way up to their late 70s, learn how to move better, ride stronger, and increase their energy. Brodie has coached top 10 Track Cyclists and Olympians to use strength training to improve their performances and reach their full potential, all while having a lot of fun and enjoying the learning process.

Holding a Bachelor's in Exercise Science from the University of Pittsburgh, a USA Cycling Expert Level Coach, SICI Certified Bike Fitter, and an NSCA CSCS with nearly 20 years of experience, Brodie offers a unique blend of considerable knowledge in exercise physiology, on-bike training, strength training, and human movement for performance.

A coffee lover, and avid learner, you'll often find coach Brodie reading while enjoying some kind of pour over coffee in his favorite mug, or the most convenient & decent local cup of joe.

Made in the USA
Las Vegas, NV
02 May 2024

89436392R00095